ESSENTIAL GUIDE
TO
SONGWRITING
PRODUCING
& RECORDING

BY DARRYL SWANN

ISBN 978-1-4768-9975-6

HAL•LEONARD®
CORPORATION
7777 W. BLUEMOUND RD. P.O. BOX 13819 MILWAUKEE, WI 53213

In Australia Contact:
Hal Leonard Australia Pty. Ltd.
4 Lentara Court
Cheltenham, Victoria, 3192 Australia
Email: ausadmin@halleonard.com.au

Visit Hal Leonard Online at
www.halleonard.com

This book is dedicated to my girls Sunnie and Savannah,
who give me a reason to keep growing; to my parents David and Marilyn,
who have always supported my dreams; and to my brothers David and Donald:
David for always exposing me to the best music and
Don who showed me how to stand up.

CONTENTS

PREFACE

Dear Reader,

Get ready to jump knee-deep into songwriting, producing, and recording. First let me share a little about myself, so you know who's writing. I have been a professional audio engineer, live sound engineer, songwriter, producer, musician, drum programmer, mixer, and – at times – mastering engineer since 1986. I say this simply to let you know that I've experienced many aspects of the music industry. Everything I write about in this book comes from real-life experience. Less theory, more hands-on, practical application.

I was never the quickest learner in school. It sometimes took me a bit longer to absorb difficult concepts, but once it clicked with me, I would zoom past the crowd like a horse that starts out the gate last, but by the end of the race is at the head of the pack. But I was always playing catch-up.

I say all this so you understand why I enjoy explaining topics in the simplest terms possible. I wish people had explained difficult concepts in simple terms when I was coming up. Many times, people like to show how smart they are by using fancy terminology. It's an ego thing.

In college, I finally realized that some teachers didn't know how to break down difficult concepts into simple, digestible terms, and many others were just outright arrogant. Many were simply stuck in an automatic pattern of spewing out the same material class after class, semester after semester, year after year.

To me, the simpler you explain yourself the better, and that is how I have written this book. Also, I've written this book both for the newbie and the consummate professional. I use many simple metaphors to illustrate complex concepts, so please indulge me if a metaphor seems far-fetched, and look for the similarities between the metaphor and the subject at hand. It will make sense in the end.

If it seems to get confusing while reading at times, just keep on reading because I always come back to the main point after taking a left turn explaining a side concept.

The three main subjects are:
- Songwriting
- Producing
- Recording

But there are many additional tidbits of juicy goodness scattered throughout the book. Please indulge me as I start out with very basic information at the beginning of the book. I simply want to start from zero for any music biz beginners. Also, I've included an appendix of emails I've exchanged with students over many years covering every subject under the sun. Thanks for checking it out, and please pass it on!

—Darryl Swann

CHAPTER 1
STYLES OF MUSIC

Because there are so many different styles of music these days, it is important to have an understanding of the main, popular styles. Let's list some of them:

- Pop
- Rock
- Urban/R&B
- Dance/Electronica
- Metal
- Rap & Hip-Hop
- Country

Let's go into all of these styles a bit. As you'll see, each branches off into many smaller groups. This is the beauty of music – it is challenging to label since producers and songwriters are always creating new styles. Each generation influences the next.

POP

Where does one start? The term "pop" is short for "popular," so whatever song reaches the widest variety of listeners is basically considered "pop music." Pop can incorporate all types of styles from Rap to Dance, Hard Rock to Urban.

Songs that become really popular – songs you might hear in a grocery store for example, are songs that may have "crossed over" into the Pop category.

ROCK

Rock branches off into various groups such as:

- Hard Rock
- Indie Rock
- Pop Rock

Usually when you think of Rock, you may think of a band – a real drummer playing real drums, a bass and guitar playing instruments hanging low, distortion on the guitar, and an overall aggressive sound. A member of the band will often begin writing a new song by introducing a guitar riff or a new melody to the rest of the band members. The "Americana" rock movement, circa 2012, breaks these traditional rock stereotypes.

URBAN/R&B

When thinking of Urban music, there is not a strong association with live musicians or a band. This style of music most often uses programmed beats and synthesizers. Songs are generally written by first programming a beat or track into a computer, a drum machine, or some other form of music software. Trap music is a new genre, a blend of electronica and southern-urban. This is a favorite of pole dancers everywhere.

DANCE ELECTRONICA

Dance/Electronica music can be broken down into smaller divisions:

- Techno
- Trance
- Drums and Bass
- Jungle
- Garage
- Dub-step
- Glitch
- Trip-hop
- Electro

This style of music has grown like crazy since the year 2000. Computer music software began to hit the market in a big way during this time. Before the year 2000, hard drives were still pretty expensive and the information passed between a computer and hard drive simply was not able to move fast enough.

Before the rise of the DAWs (digital audio workstations; e.g., Pro Tools, Logic, Reason, etc.) circa the year 2000, electronic music was primarily created using stand-alone drum-machines and keyboard sequencers.

Electronica (electronic music) first appeared in the 1970s, created by groups like Kraftwerk. In writing an Electronica song, a producer or programmer often begins with a repeating melody line and builds the beat around it, or by creating the beat first and then writing the song around the beat.

METAL

Metal, or Heavy Metal, branches off into smaller categories. A few main styles are:

- Original Metal (Black Sabbath)
- Death Metal (Morbid Angel)
- New Metal (Deftones)
- Speed Metal (Motorhead)

Metal is usually loud and distorted. Yeah! Like Rock, Metal songs are many times born by a member of the band introducing a cool riff or small melody of some type to his band mates. Each person may then create his own part for his particular instrument.

Sometimes the person in the band who writes the lyrics may come up with a cool melodic singing line and then the band will fit chords around it. In my experience, most bands write songs together. No matter what style, there is no one way to approach songwriting.

Many people credit Ozzy Osborne's first band, Black Sabbath, among a few others, for inventing Heavy Metal.

RAP & HIP-HOP

Everyone asks, "What's the difference between rap and hip-hop?" Many different people have many varying explanations as to the difference between the two.

You can think of the term Hip-Hop as describing an entire way of living: rapping, break dancing, graffiti art, DJ-ing, and all the other doings that go along with these activities; how the people who do these things dress, the slang words they use, and so on can all be thought of as a kind of way of life, a culture. Hip-Hop culture.

Rapping is a part of this way of life. So, in essence, the terms Hip-Hop and Rap are synonymous. They mean the same thing. There are, however, the true-to-heart fans and artists who say that Hip-Hop music is the real-deal style that never makes it to the radio and that Rap music is the more pop-sounding of the two. It's all relative at the end of the day.

Hip-Hop/Rap music breaks out into different variations as well. Some of the main types, and artists, bands, are:

- East Coast (KRS-One; Wu-Tang)
- West Coast (Snoop Dogg)
- Dirty South (Lil-Jon)
- Northern/Great Lakes (Slum Village; J-Dilla)
- Miami (Luke Skyywalker)
- Northern Cali (DJ Quik; Too $hort)

Just like Electronica, writing a Rap/Hip-Hop song usually begins with making the beat. Many times though, rappers (or MCs, which means Master of Ceremonies) will write lyrics without any beat and will simply store the lyrics in a notebook until he or she comes across the right music track.

By "track," we mean a beat with musical layers on top. By "beat," we're usually referring to the programmed drums with very few musical layers added. But the words "track" and "beat" are often used synonymously.

COUNTRY MUSIC

We all know what Country music sounds like, or at least we think we do. More often than not, we may think of someone singing in a twangy, Southern accent to a slide guitar. Someone else might say that it sounds melancholy. These are stereotypes.

Country music is a traditional style of American music that has undergone many transformations. Traditional Country music is a blend of Bluegrass, Gospel, Blues, and folk music. Country, like the other types of music so far listed, breaks out into many different forms. To name just a few, we have:

- Honky Tonk
- Country Rock
- Rockabilly
- Pop-Country
- Country Soul, Bluegrass, and others

Country music usually has well-written lyrics and singable, catchy melodies. Country songs many times begin with the lyrics and melody written first, with the instrumental and vocal harmonies added later.

CHAPTER 2
SONGWRITING BASICS

APPROACHING SONGWRITING

If you intend to go after your dream of success in the music biz, it is important to have a basic understanding of the different styles listed in Chapter 1. You want to keep an objective mind and a wide perspective.

Many times, we don't know how to begin writing that hit song, so let's break this down and make some suggestions. Here's a short list of ways to begin:

- Chordally
- Beat-driven
- Sound-driven
- Lyrics and/or melodies

Don't just skip over these four different possible ways of how to start writing a song. Take a moment and think about each one. Ponder what each one means. These are key points in understanding various ways to begin writing. Trust me, each method will create a unique production style at the end of the day. Think of this as choosing the DNA of the production style of your song. How you start can make a huge difference in the end.

Starting a Song Chordally

Writing a song chordally means to start messing around on the guitar or piano. Begin by playing a few notes or chords, one after the other until you find a combination that sounds catchy. Even if you are not a musician, per se, just try noodling around. Don't think too much, just tinker around.

This small cluster of notes or chords is the DNA for your song. Once you feel you have found a few note combinations or chords you like, keep messing around with them by switching up the order you play them and how fast or slow you play them. Play them up high, then down low. After a few hours, you will have figured out the right combination and speed. I repeat, just start fiddling around. Don't think too much. More on this later.

Starting a Song by Finding a Cool Beat

Usually Urban/R&B, Rap, Pop, and even some Rock begins with first creating a cool beat. The terms "beat" and "track" both really mean the same thing, but to be more specific, a track usually refers to a beat with more musical layers on it.

But, even a beat can sound really cool by itself. Tracks and beats are created either by a drum machine like the AKAI-MPC, or in a music software program like Pro Tools, Logic, Garage Band, Studio One, Reason, Ableton, FL Studio, and others.

Lastly, there is a difference between the word "beat," which is a general, generic term for something that has rhythm to it – the way an alarm clock may have a rhythmic pattern to its ring – as opposed to our term "beat," which refers to a cool, crafted rhythm we create for a singer or rapper.

These kind of beats need to have unique, even odd-sounding, elements. This means the snare drum, kick drum, percussion sounds, and bass line each need to sound special, maybe even a little weird.

For example, if you hit a real snare drum, it will sound like a snare drum, right? Duh. But, if you hit the snare drum in the bathroom while flushing the toilet, this background noise is going to create a crazy swooshing sound behind the snare.

Of course, you will know what's going on, but someone who does not know what you did will probably say, "Whoa! That sounds different. Where did you get that snare? May I copy it?" As silly as my example is, this probably would be your friend's comment after hearing this snare sound recorded while flushing the toilet.

Think outside the box! Each drum sound you use in a beat should make the listener say, "I wonder how he found that kick drum, snare drum, etc."

Starting a Song by Finding a Cool Sound

If you scroll through all of the sounds in a keyboard, you will obviously stumble across a few sounds that really catch your ear because the sound itself is spooky, sad, mad, excited, loving, or evokes other emotions. That is what I mean by "sound-driven."

For example, the sound of a deep church bell in the distance might make a person feel warm and fuzzy because it reminds them of going to church on Sunday with family. Another person might find the sound scary, like an old Dracula movie. The point here is that the sound itself – its tone color – tells an entire story without even playing a bunch of notes or chords.

Now that anyone with a DAW (digital audio workstation) like Pro Tools, Logic, Reason, Nuendo, FL Studio, Ableton, or Studio One has access to virtual synthesizers built right into the program, they are much more likely to find stimulating, interesting sounds. It just takes a little time and some patience to sift through the multitude of sounds in each of these programs.

Once you have found a really cool sound, see how it makes you feel. What emotion does it spark in you? Anger? Love? Humor? Fear? If you are able to identify an emotion, you are halfway there. More on this later.

Beginning a Song with Lyrics and/or Melodies

Many songs are born from lyrics and/or melodies. Country music is driven by storytelling, which means many Country songs begin with lyrics.

A songwriter may start by humming a melody without words, knowing that if he perfects the melody in his head, the lyrics will come. Another writer may have a catchy phrase with no melody, knowing that a tune will come as he adds more words to the ones he already has.

A simple phrase like, "All the king's men" may be bouncing around in your head for a day or two and you do not know how it got there! This happens to me all the time. By subconsciously repeating it in my head, new thoughts like, "Who are the king's men?" "What do they look like?" "How many are out there?" are born.

Sometimes I have trouble getting my brain to think of something else! So, if you are an obsessive person who tends to focus on things without even trying, you are blessed with a great gift. If I consciously plant an idea in my head, my brain will automatically start working on it as I go about my day. When I revisit the idea in my head later, my brain always produces results. Magically, I have new ideas whenever I do this. You can do this too. It works. Sounds crazy, huh? Try it.

Once you have a few strong phrases strung together and a melody worked out, chords can easily be put to them. Any decent musician can find the right chords to accompany the lyrics and melodies.

Lastly, I want to stress that there is a difference between lyrics and prose/poetry. I run across many people who write poetry who think their poems can become lyrics to a song. Poetry tends to be a bit more intricate and wordier than lyrics. Poetry is usually read by itself, whereas lyrics must work well with the music both melodically and rhythmically.

The musical style of "spoken word" is where poetry is read over live music. The poet is free to ebb and flow above the music, and both poet and band feed off each other. For example, if the poet gets loud in a section, the band may grow in intensity behind him/her and vice versa.

In a song, the lyrics have been groomed to blend with the music as if it were an instrument. Lyrics are much more synchronized with the music as opposed to spoken word being much looser.

WHAT SHOULD I WRITE ABOUT?

That's a good question. Do some thinking: What significant things have happened in your life during the past three to six months? Did someone have a baby? Did you win some money? Did you fall in or out of love, see a good movie, read a really great book that sparked your thinking in any way? If you ask yourself and really think about it, many potential song topics will pop up.

Let's put lyrics writing into two subject categories:
- Trendy
- Timeless

Trendy lyrics usually use Hip-Hop slang words or reflect something that is happening now in the world, like a popular person getting into trouble or use of a slang phrase like "swagger" or whatever. These types of songs usually get popular fast then fade after a month or even a couple of weeks.

Timeless songs tend to speak of more universal themes such as love, religion, drama, emotions, etc. It does not matter whether you hear a timeless song today or 20 years from now. It will always be relevant because there will always be central themes common to everyone and every era. It is important to know, however, that even if the sentiments your lyrics express are timeless, the sounds you use for instruments can date your song.

We all know what '80s music sounds like:
- Artificial-sounding drums
- Lots of echo and reverb
- Somewhat nerdy
- Cheap-sounding keyboards

Don't get me wrong. I love the retro 1980s sounds and revival happening as I write this book some 30 years later. But be conscious of the fact that using sounds that are associated with a certain time period may put your song in a category you may not want it to be in.

CHAPTER 3
SONG STRUCTURE

ANATOMY OF A SONG

Here we are going to discuss the various sections used in songs. Just as a car is made up of many different parts – wheels, engine, frame, dashboard – songs contain many different combinations of parts as well.

Intro

Pretty simple – the beginning of the song. The **intro** usually has fewer musical layers than other parts of the song. On the other hand, it might be really huge in order to shock the listener and get his attention.

Intros sometimes have lyrics without music, music without lyrics, music and lyrics, music and melodies only, or any other way one can think of to start a song that will capture the listener's attention. Choruses sometimes act as intros where the song will begin with the chorus and then go into verse one.

Chorus

The **chorus** is the central idea of the story of the song. It contains the memorable melody.

Verse(s)

The **verses** tell the story. Think of each verse as a different chapter. Generally, contemporary commercial songs have two to three verses.

B section or Pre-Chorus

The **B section** usually comes between the verses and choruses; connects verses and choruses together.

Bridge

Many times the **bridge** comes after the second chorus. The first verse lays out a chapter of our story, then the chorus/hook comes in and paraphrases the story into a catchy phrase. Then the second verse comes back in with another episode or chapter of the story, then perhaps a B section, then the second chorus sums it up again.

Next, the **bridge** comes in and may state how we intend to fix the problem we have been expressing in the verses and choruses, what change in behavior we intend to make in order to make things better for us. Bridges also may offer a new point of view as to what is happening in the story. At the end of the day, though, there are no strict rules; these are just some general guidelines for you to follow if you wish.

Tag

Tag is a slang word for the section that may come right after the chorus. Think of it as an alternate chorus. Tags are great "ear candy," like two sweet hooks back to back.

Vamp/Outro

Vamp is another slang term that usually refers to the very end of a song. Vamps add interest to the song by bringing in more background vocals, more instruments, transposing the song (modulating: going to a higher key for dramatic effect), or any other way to add more intensity to the end of the song.

Gospel songs are a good example of this: they may speed up at the very end and send the crowd into a frenzy. Vamps always work, but don't use them too often. I'd say one song per every five. Having vamps on too many songs will diminish the overall intended effect. Your project will start to sound gimmicky and too formulated.

Solo

Duh! We all know what that is. **Solos** showcase a particular instrument in a section with a fancy or simple display of talent. They are also effective for either reinforcing the chorus/hook melody, or for introducing a new, catchy melody.

Breakdown

A **breakdown** is where all the music drops out and only the beat is heard. Sometimes one instrument is left in with the beat. Breakdowns are great for creating contrast so that when the music does come back, it sounds huge.

To make it clear, a chorus and a hook often mean the same thing, though they may have other meanings as well. The word **chorus** usually refers to the overall chorus section, where the term **hook** can sometimes mean the one line in the chorus that is the most memorable part of the chorus, the line everyone knows. If you were to sing the hook to someone, they would most likely recognize the song.

SONG STRUCTURES

Popular songs usually have simple song structures. By song structure, we mean the order in which you put together these individual parts one after the other (verse, chorus, bridge, etc.).

Let's take a look at some typical song structures. There is no right or wrong way to structure a song, but usually the simpler it is, the better your chances of reaching a bigger audience.

Key:

C = chorus

V = verse

B = B section/pre-chorus

BR = bridge

T = tag

VP = vamp/outro

I = intro

S = solo

BD = breakdown

STRUCTURE 1

I – V1 – C1 – V2 – C2 – BR – C3 – End

STRUCTURE 2

Intro C – V1 – B1 – C1 – V2 – B2 – C2 – BR – BD – C3 – VP

STRUCTURE 3

V1 – C1 – Tag – V2 – B – C2 – Tag – BR – C3 – Tag – VP

There is an unlimited number of variations of song structures. This is what makes song writing so fun and so challenging! These are just three examples of many, many different potential combinations. Structure 1 is obviously the most basic of the three shown.

Each section of a song has a certain length. We count section length in terms of bars (measures). Most of you know what a bar is, but for those of you who are not familiar, no problem. It is essential you understand bars and beats. Generally-speaking, one **bar** (measure) is equal to four taps. So to count bars, you'd say: "**One**, two, three, four; **two**, two, three, four; **three**, two, three, four; **four**, two, three, four; **five**, two, three, four," and so forth. By the way, we just counted five bars.

In contemporary pop music, many sections are either four or eight bars each. This allows the listener to follow without too many complex turns and changes. Jazz and classical music tend to have many different bar-length combinations.

CHAPTER 4
HOW TO WRITE A SONG

LET'S BEGIN

Now that we understand some basics regarding how songs are put together, let's take a stab at writing a song. In Chapter 2, I laid out four different ways to spark the writing of a song:

- *Chord driven.* Have you been messing around with a few notes or chords on the guitar or piano?
- *Beat driven.* Have you been tinkering with a beat?
- *Sound driven.* Have you stumbled upon a killer sound in a synth on your computer?
- *Lyrics/Melody Driven.* Do you or your partner have some lyrics brewin'? A cool story to tell? A catchy hook phrase, possibly?

Whichever of these you may have, start there! When being creative, it is always best to jump right into it without thinking too much about it. Too much thinking often slows you down. There is an old phrase that fits in perfectly here: "The paralysis of analysis." This means that there is too much thinking and not enough action!

Once you have created one of these four sparks, open up a click track in your computer music program (Studio One, GarageBand, Logic, Pro Tools, Reason, FL Studio, etc.) and document the idea. By *document the idea*, I mean to record what you have, as it is.

You may have only a few chords, a rough beat, a cool synth sound, or lyric/melody idea. It's okay if the song is not fully thought out. The important thing is to lay it down in a session so you can begin to think of other parts to add to flesh out the song.

If you don't have any of these four sparks already in motion, it is time to get one going! Here are some tips on how to get this ball moving:

Grab a guitar or get on a keyboard and just start fiddling. It is sometimes helpful to skip randomly through the radio dial for a few minutes or scroll through your iTunes to get your creative juices going. I don't mean copy someone else's music! I mean scroll quickly past a few stations just to tickle your ears and brain.

Scroll through some drum loops. See if there is a groove that moves you. Don't think about each loop too much, just scroll through a library of loops. Whichever ones get you thinking right away, drag these into your session and build bass, guitar, and/or keyboard parts on top of the loop.

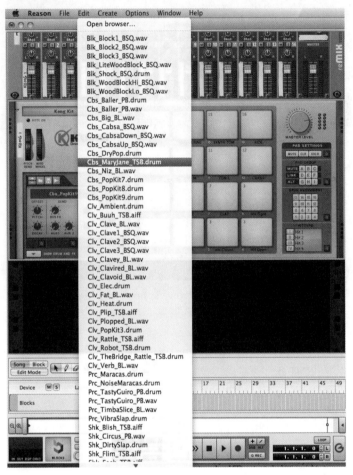

If you do not play an instrument, find a buddy who does and feed him ideas (and pizza) of what you want him to play to the loop. Invite him to play:

- Something heavy and mean
- Something light and happy
- Something jazzy
- Something with lots of rhythm

You will be surprised at what you pull out of him creatively when you offer some direction. (This is what a producer does.)

Get on a cool synthesizer, or open a keyboard in your DAW (digital audio workstation: Studio One, Reason, Logic, Pro Tools, etc.). You do not need to be a keyboardist simply to scroll through the sounds in these synthesizers.

Just like the drum loops, scroll through the synth sounds until you find one that touches you, one that evokes a mood for you. Again, don't think too much! Just listen and feel. "A great sound will inspire an entire song."

If you have only a *melody*, try to find a few chords that go along with it. It is always cool to write with another person or even a few other people. You will be surprised at how many ideas will be sparked.

If you have *lyrics* only, try repeating them over and over in a rhythmic way. Eventually, you will get a feel for how the rhythm of the lyrics should sound. Once this happens, melodies will begin to present themselves, especially if you are bouncing your ideas off of others in the room with you.

If you start out with both *lyrics* and *melodies*, it will be that much easier to put them to music. If you don't feel you have the best ear in finding chords on guitar or piano, collaborate with someone who does. Again, you will be surprised at how easily ideas begin to flow. Once this happens, you will be hooked forever.

DOCUMENT INITIAL ELEMENTS TO SCRATCH TRACK

As stated above, to *document* something, means to *record* it. Instead of focusing on the best way to record it, do it without too much thought. It's like drawing a pencil sketch of something: You are not going for accuracy; you are just getting the preliminary idea across.

Once you feel you have one of these:
- Some cool chords worked out
- A cool drumbeat going
- Found a great synth sound
- The beginnings of some great lyrics and/or melody

...Then – open up a new session in your DAW and put your idea down. Record it! Don't wait. Even though you might not have the whole thing worked out, go ahead and record. Even if you have only a small cluster of three notes on a keyboard as your idea, open up a click track in your DAW, find a comfortable tempo for these three notes, then record yourself playing these three notes over and over for about a minute or so.

CONTINUE TO WRITE SONG TO COMPLETION

Writing with others is a great way to build your song out and discover new ideas. I strongly suggest everyone try it! You might have to try out a few different people before you find folks you really enjoy writing with. Trust me, you'll run into some real knuckleheads on the way.

If you are a music writer – that is, you write the chords or make the beat – you will want to find a good lyricist/melody writer. You may also want to work with other "chord" people as well. As I said, you'll be surprised at what you come up with creatively when you collaborate with others.

HOW TO PROCEED WITH CO-WRITERS

Play what you have so far for your co-writer, even if it is far from complete. If you have an idea of what is missing from your song, tell the co-writer what you are thinking of, but allow the co-writer to be creative and do his own thing.

Try not to be a dictator and overly controlling in what it is you might be hearing for the song. At the same time, if what the co-writer is coming up with is very different from where you want the song to go, tell the co-writer that creatively he/she is too far from where you hear the song needs to go. Try to find a happy compromise. Be sincere. It always makes a difference.

Continue to add musical layers to the initial scratch tracks until the song begins to develop. Make sure to be a filter, though – you don't need to keep every idea the co-writer comes up with. It is okay not to use every idea.

WHEN AM I DONE?

The million dollar question is, "How will I know when the songwriting is complete?" You are not alone asking this question! A good way is to get away from the song. Don't listen to it for a few days. When you do listen to it again, you will know in your heart if it is complete or not. The sections in the song that still need work will really stand out to you at this point.

Don't worry if you do not fully trust your own judgment yet. Songwriting is a cumulative process; the more you do it, the more natural the process becomes. In the meantime, compare your work-in-progress to a song or production you like. Using a reference is a great learning tool.

If you are still not sure if it is done, ask a few people who are not attached to the song to listen and see what they think.

BUT BEWARE...

Most people will hear the raw documented sounds you are playing around with and think that they are the finished sounds. They will not be hearing the actual quality of the song itself because the production (better sounds and perfected parts) has not yet been done.

Once you feel that the raw layers have set a clear enough picture of how the song should sound, you are done writing the song and are ready to record the song for real. Now that the chords, the tempo, the lyrics, and melodies are all figured out, it is now time to go back and replace the rough sounds with better-sounding and better-played parts.

Also, it is time to have a singer give a killer performance and sing the lyrics and melodies as if their life depends on it! The rough vocal ideas you used while figuring it all out does not showcase the lyrics/melodies to their fullest.

The next step between writing the song and recording the song for real is to be aware of what a record producer does. We will dig into this in the next chapter, but first let's finish this songwriting chapter by looking at how to split the ownership of a song between the co-writers.

SPLITTING OWNERSHIP OF A SONG

Trust me, there is no perfect formula as to how to go about splitting up a song! Let's start with some basics.

A traditional way of viewing ownership of a song:
- 50 percent music (chord changes and/or track)
- 50 percent lyrics and melody

Whoever participated in creating the chord changes and/or track gets a piece of the 50 percent music side. Whoever participated in writing the lyrics (words) and/or the melody gets a piece of the 50 percent lyrics/melody side.

Please note: There is a huge difference between someone who actually thinks up the chords for a song as opposed to a musician you bring in at the end who takes the chords already written and then re-records them for you with sweeter sounds and performances. This second person is not a writer of the song – they are a performer on the song.

Let's say there are only three chords in the entire song written by Roscoe. Then, Sebastian is asked to come in and make these three chords sound cool. Sebastian comes in with a great selection of guitars and a sweet pedal board with tons of guitar effects. He makes those three chords sound really incredible. Even though Sebastian made those three simple chords sound like so much more, he is not a writer, but only a performer on the song. The performer does not receive any royalties. Only the writer gets royalties.
- Writer: gets a piece of ownership of song (copyright)
- Performer: gets paid at a session for his playing and gets a credit on the record ("Guitar by Sebastian"); receives no royalties

There are always exceptions, though. Roscoe (songwriter) may offer Sebastian (guitar player) a small piece of ownership because he contributed such an incredible performance and made the song so much more than it was. Technically though, the guitar player is entitled only to money for his performance and time, and is credited on the final product.

What is a Royalty?

A **royalty** is a payment to someone who owns a piece – or all – of a song when that song is sold on a record, purchased as a digital copy online, or is played on the radio or TV (public performance). In essence, the person is paid when the song is transacted commercially in some way.

A payment may come from a radio station that pays the songwriter each time the radio station plays the song on the air. It may also come from a record label, among other places. For example, if Celine Dion records a song written by you and puts it on her album, she is really just renting the song from you; every time she sells a record with your song on it, she (her label) has to pay you some "rent," which is otherwise known as a **mechanical royalty**.

What is a Copyright?

Copyright is a fancy word that denotes who it is that owns and controls the use of a given song. A mistake people commonly make is thinking that the copyright office (Library of Congress in D.C.) issues copyrights. Not true! The copyright office in Washington D.C. only offers copyright-registration/protection. They are really just acting as a witness of something you are claiming is yours.

Here is an example. Let's say you have some lyrics and a cool melody in your head. You sing them for people and they love 'em, but you have not recorded them yet.

Once you record the lyrics and melody, you actually own that recording, correct? Correct! Since you own the rights to that one copy, you now own the "copy right." It is that simple. You have total control over who you let make copies/duplicates of that original recording.

But let's say someone hears your original recording and takes the idea and creates their own version of your lyrics and melodies? If you have not protected the idea by having someone else witness the fact that you created it on a given day, then that person can claim it is theirs.

So before you let too many people hear the recording, you want to protect yourself to prove you came up with the idea first. The way you prove this is by having a witness/entity listen to it first before anyone else. That way, you can call on them to confirm the day you let them hear the original. This is what the Library of Congress/ Copyright Office in Washington D.C. does: They issue copyright registration. They are a witness that you created the idea on a given day.

In conclusion, don't feel like you cannot let anyone hear your music before it is protected, but be cautious of who you give a copy to before protected. Protecting your material with the Library of Congress costs some money, about $35–$100 to protect one or more titles. http://www.copyright.gov

CHAPTER 5
WHAT IS A PRODUCER?

A producer has many jobs in producing a music project. A few of the most important roles are knowing how to:

- Execute pre-production really well.
- Identify cool sounds.
- Motivate musicians and singers to perform their very best when recording their parts on a song.

In a nutshell, a producer must know how to organize and motivate people. Let's go through these three points in more detail.

PRE-PRODUCTION.
WHAT THE HECK IS IT?

Pre- means before. *Production* means recording for real. When I am writing a song, I am not necessarily focused on what my guitar sounds like or how well I play the chords. I am more attuned to figuring out the chords and to creating the best song possible.

After the song is written – i.e., a rough recording of the song like a pencil sketch – it is then time to re-record. Essentially, we replace the pencil-sketch sounds with really cool sounds and play those parts really well. This is what we mean by "recording for real."

Back to pre-production. As I said, it means "before we record." So prior to going into a fancy studio, we must make sure the song is the best it can be. We must create a plan regarding the best way to record it. For example:

- If the song was initiated with a drum loop from a machine, are we going to add live drums?
- Are we going to record all of the musicians at the same time or one at a time?
- Which musicians will do the best job? Do we need to scout around for a guitarist who has a certain playing style or who has a huge pedal board of effects?

- Are we going to have the drummer play to a click track so that he stays in time better or let him play freely, which will give the song a more "live" feel?
- Can our drummer even play to a click track? (It is not the easiest thing to do well.)
- What studio are we going to use? Are we going to record the drums at a bigger studio where we can use more microphones, then go back to our home studio and record all the other elements/instruments one at a time?

There are many options to think about, but I don't want it to sound too complicated. It really comes down to some basic, common-sense decisions. If you just take a moment and think each song through, the best plan will come to you.

Consider the overall sound you want the song to have. Think of a song by a band you like and use that song's sound as a reference for the way you want your song to sound. I don't mean for you to copy the same chords, but to think of the overall mood the song has. For instance:

- Do the guitars sound smooth and polished or are they ratty like Punk-Rock?
- Are the drums big as if they are being played in a stadium, or do they have no echo and sound tight and dry as if played in a padded closet?

Think of how you want each element (instrument) in your production to sound and how you want it played by the musician. Once you know the overall sound of the song you want, pick each instrument apart in your head and imagine how it should sound.

This goes for the vocals as well. Do you want the vocals to be raw and aggressive like Punk Rock or Gangsta Rap, or smooth and polished like R&B dance music with lots of background vocals coming in and out around the lead vocal?

It is your job as the producer to let the singer know how you want him/her to sing the lead vocal and whether or not you want him/her to do background vocals. If backing vocals are desired, help the singers come up with these parts.

CHAPTER 6
PRE-PRODUCTION

GETTING PRE-PRODUCTION STARTED

Now that we've looked at how the producer must have an overall vision of the song(s), let's begin the process in earnest. The first step is critical listening. It is time for you to first make sure the song itself is the best it can be before you jump into thinking of the overall product and the sound of each instrument.

Critical listening means that you try to tear the song apart to see if it stands up – like car companies doing crash tests to see how durable their product is before they paint it and make it look all fancy. How do we do this? Let's list five ways:

- Lyrics
- Melody
- Structure
- Tempo
- Key

LYRICS

The good news is that, as a producer, I don't really need to fix anyone's lyrics. I just need to point out to the writer when the lyrics are bad. But remember, creativity is of course purely subjective, meaning there is no right or wrong. Everyone has an opinion when it comes to creativity. Still, in my opinion there are a couple of things that usually make lyrics bad:

- Too many clichés
- Wordiness

What is a cliché?

A *cliché* is a phrase we have all heard before. For example: a penny for your thoughts; actions speak louder than words; save the drama for your mama. In writing lyrics, a cliché is a phrase that is just too convenient. I call these throwaway lyrics. For example, I was working with an artist who wrote this hook:

I know all your true colors:
Yellow, green, black, and white.
I know all your true colors.
Yeah, that's right.

I challenged the artist to come up with a different fourth line because it was a throw-away lyric. She came up with this:

I know all your true colors:
Yellow, green, black, and white.
I know all your true colors,
Like the back of my hand, that's no lie…

The new line – "Like the back of my hand, that's no lie" – was so much better than what she had prior. If you know someone as well as you know the back of your hand, then you are telling the listener something important instead of just throwing out a generic rhyme.

In conclusion, many hit songs use clichés here and there. They can be an effective tool for creating catchy hooks, but be aware of two things regarding clichés:

- Too many clichés strung together
- Throwaway lines

What is wordiness?

Have you ever heard lyrics that sound more like a Shakespearean sonnet than song lyrics? There is a difference between poetry and song lyrics. Here is an example of wordiness: *The lightning in the sky reminds me of the eloquence of your heart, because when you share your feelings, it sets off a spark that says that my love shows the impression of desert sands.*

How ridiculous! The words just go on and on and at the end you really don't even know what is being said. The best lyrics are straight-ahead in their meaning. They're conversational, as if the singer is telling you a story at dinner. The story should be interesting, not confusing.

MELODY

The second way to pick a song apart is to see if the song has a melody that the listener may remember. A memorable melody is so very important! A good example is "Happy Birthday to You." You could not forget this melody even if you tried.

If the style of music you are working on is Rap – or something like Death-Metal, where the singer is screaming – then it is important that the music contain some musical hooks instead of vocal hooks.

STRUCTURE

A third way to pick apart a song is by analyzing its structure. By this, we mean two things:

- The order of the sections of the song
- The overall length of the song

For example, if a certain section of a song – let's say the verse – repeats itself over and over before moving on to the next section, the listener is probably going to get bored with it. We prefer variety, whether it is food, movies, conversation, etc.

We get bored easily. The same goes for listening to a song. My general rule for songs: the shorter the better.

As a critical listener, endeavor to hear the song as if it were your first time. Clear your mind and stop any random thinking bouncing around in your head. Try taking a few deep, cleansing breaths just before listening. See if you think any section of the song goes on for too long. Feel the song as you listen to it. Don't think. Feel! If you do get bored with a section, suggest to the writer or the artist that the section perhaps should be shortened, or made more compelling in some way.

TEMPO

The fourth way to analyze a song is determine whether the tempo is right. *Tempo* refers to the beats per minute (bpm) of the song. To give you an idea of general BPMs of different styles of music, here is a basic chart:

- 60–70 bpm   Ballad/Love Song
- 75–90 bpm   Classic Rock (e.g., Led Zeppelin)
- 95–105 bpm   R&B/Urban music
- 115–140 bpm   Electro dance music
- 150–180 bpm   Drum & Bass Electronica

When we first documented (recorded) the song idea in the beginning, we were not clear what the idea would blossom into. We were not focused on capturing the perfect tempo. We just wanted to get the idea down first. Now that the idea has grown into the beginnings of a really cool song, it is important that we now go back and get all the details right – like the tempo.

Making sure the tempo is right for the song is not necessarily the easiest thing to do. If the rough version of the song is moving too fast or too slow, it might not be readily apparent. It takes a bit of concentration to figure out a proper tempo.

Sometimes the tempo of the rough idea is good. At other times, the rough idea may seem to drag a bit. In that case, we should speed it up so it doesn't sound sluggish. On the other hand, we may have a song that has a cool dance groove to it; we may need to slow it down to let the groove "swing" more.

If you do not believe you have found the correct tempo for your song, have the drummer play to a click track at a faster or slower tempo until it feels right to you. Walk around the room to the beat as the drummer (or drum machine) is playing. As you do this, you will instinctively feel whether or not you are bobbing your head up and down in a comfortable way. Speed up the click a few BPMs, walk to it for a minute, then slow it down a few BPMs and walk. You'll know when it feels right. If you try to determine the best tempo for the song only by listening to the original scratch tempo, your frame of reference is limited – so walk! The skill of determining good tempo comes with time; the more you do it, the more intuitive your senses become.

THE KEY OF THE SONG

The final way to pick a song apart is to determine – like Goldilocks – whether the key of the song is too high, too low, or just right. To do this, listen to the lead vocal. If the singer is straining to reach the top notes throughout the song, you may want to try playing it a note or two lower. Also, ascertain whether the singer is having difficulty hitting the top notes in the melody of the song itself or only various ad lib notes at the end of the song. If the trouble is with the latter, then you do not necessarily need to change the key of the song. Change the ad libs in the vamp.

On the other hand, if the song is too low, the singer may bottom out. This often pertains to female singers. Sometimes a song is too low for a woman to hit many of the notes, and she is not able to sing with power. Play the song a step or two higher so she is in her comfortable singing range.

BAND OR SOLO ARTIST?

Now that you have picked the song apart by analyzing:

- Lyrics
- Melody
- Structure
- Tempo
- Key

…and have figured out some ways to make the song better, it is now time to think about how you are going to record the song "for real."

As mentioned earlier, step one of writing the song is only the rough draft. After you write it, then you need to re-record it for real using:

- Better-sounding instruments
- Better-performed parts
- A great vocal performance and background vocals (if need be)
- The ideas you discovered on how to make the lyrics/ melodies/structure/tempo and key better for the song

One of the first things to think about is whether this song is intended for a band, or a solo artist. Let's take a look at these for a moment.

Band

Here are some steps on how to get a band ready to record the song "for real" in the studio.

Before you go into the studio, rent a cheap rehearsal hall or set up in someone's garage. Have the band incorporate all the new ideas on how to make the songs better. It's useful to break down the rehearsal schedule in several steps:

- Have the band rehearse the song with the new tempo (using a metronome; drummer puts earpiece in), new song structure if any, and new key if changed. This step may take a day or two of repetition to get them tight. Be diligent in making sure band members are focused during rehearsals and are truly absorbing these changes to the songs.

- Next (day three), have only the drummer and the bass player perform together to make sure the kick-drum pattern is in sync with the bass pattern. Any discrepancies between kick and bass line should be fixed. As soon as you hear a divergence, stop them and see if bass line is clashing with drummer's kick pattern, or vice versa.

- Day four of rehearsals: Create cool parts for each instrument/member. For example, the guitar player might be playing the same rhythm over and over throughout the song. Suggest that he play arpeggios in one section instead of just chunking hard all the time. This goes for any musician/band member you feel is playing the same repetitious part all the way from the beginning of the song till the end. Boring! A good way to stimulate new parts is to ask a musician to play the exact opposite of what he is doing. Ask him to just indulge you and try.

- Day 6 (or possibly 7): Now that you have some new ways to play the different sections of the song, make sure the band can play the entire song from top to bottom smoothly, without mistakes. Having the band rehearse the song(s) over and over will make the music feel more natural to them.

- Why is it that every member of every band feels inclined to take a two-second solo at the same time at every transition, from verse to chorus or chorus to bridge (etc.), in every song? This is when you go from being a producer to a reducer. Make sure each member plays simply from section to section, with minimal embellishment, so that when the song needs some climax, they have not given all their aces away earlier.

When you finally go into the recording studio with the band, they will be able to perform the songs well by putting their hearts and souls into their parts without having to think too much.

If someone is thinking about his part too much in the recording studio, he is not going to play as well, because it will not feel like second nature. The same is true for a band playing a gig. You can always tell whether or not a band has rehearsed enough. If they haven't, they will be looking at each other onstage with puzzled expressions on their faces. Obviously, they are not giving their best performance to the audience!

The same rule applies for going into the recording studio. The puzzled looks should be reserved for the rehearsals. The recording studio is where they should be giving their very best performance.

Solo Artist

Let's break this term down into two categories:

1. Singer/songwriter. John Mayer, Alanis Morissette – these artists wrote their own songs, but usually did not have a band when they first started. John Mayer could play his songs on guitar, but did not have a band when he first got signed. A producer helped him add the layers to his songs to create the cool, layered, produced sound of his first record.

2. Performing artist. Britney Spears, Celine Dion, Janet Jackson, Diana Ross, and Frank Sinatra – all of these singers fall fit into this category. These artists did not write their own songs. They sang songs written by producers and songwriters and relied on their producer to create their sound, helping them determine whether their music would sound dancy, Hard-Rock, R&Bish, or whatever.

These performing artists are known for their vocal styles, looks, and personalities as opposed to singer/songwriters who are also known for the lyrics they write and the stories they tell. Since a solo artist does not have a band per se, most likely you are going to work on the songs in your DAW, (Pro Tools, Studio One, Logic, Cubase, etc.). There is no need to rent a rehearsal studio.

But regardless of whether you are working with a band or a solo artist, the song still comes first. This means that we need to either write or find a song for the performing artist to sing that will represent his or her musical direction. Once you find or write a song, then it is time to pick the song apart using the five categories:

- Lyrics
- Melody
- Structure
- Tempo
- Key

The same applies to a singer/songwriter's self-written songs. Once you determine which ones to move forward with, you subject those songs to the same scrutiny using the five criteria listed above.

You need to tweak each song for the solo artist so it fits just right for them. If you don't analyze the songs using these steps, you will miss the opportunity to make each song the best it can be for that particular artist. It is a way of customizing each song for the artist.

After tweaking and customizing the songs for the solo artist, determine the best way to go about recording the songs "for real." Here are just a few different ways you could do this. Take a moment and think about each one:

- Re-create all the music in the DAW using better-sounding, hand-picked internal sounds.

- Record real drums, then add all the other sounds using internal keyboards from the DAW.
- Create programmed drums in the DAW, then record live musicians to create the various layers of the production.
- Use all live musicians to re-create the song. This way, you (producer) need to guide each musician as to how you want them to play each part.

Remember, this is not a band that has its own ideas. You are hiring these musicians to come in and play how you want the song to turn out in the end. These musicians you bring in are not writers of the song; they are performers. They are entitled to compensation for their time and a credit on the final product. Their contribution is "work for hire," so they receive no royalty from the sale of the song(s).

There are many different ways to approach laying the song down for the solo artist. If you visualize how you want the song to sound when it's all done, it will help you determine how to go about executing each layer you record. Think it through.

Be open to listening to songs by famous bands and artists you like and use their sound as a reference for how you want your production to sound.

Listen to each instrument, each vocal layer, and try to figure out how they did it. This is a huge help in understanding how to build the layers in your song.

RECORDING THE SONGS "FOR REAL"

It is time to record the songs for real when:

- The songs are written.
- The pre-production process of tearing the songs apart by analyzing lyrics, melody, song structure, tempo, and key has taken place.
- The band has worked in a rehearsal space and the songs have been practiced with all the new changes.

    OR

- You've figured out how the songs should sound for the solo artist.

When you begin this process, the primary focus should be on two things:

- Getting the best performances out of each musician and singer who performs on the final versions.
- Getting the best sound for each layer you add to each song.

Let's go into each of these in more detail:

In terms of musicians and singers who perform on your production/song, it is the producer's job first to let each performer know what is expected of him, then motivate each player into giving the best performance he can. Most musicians truly want to do their best, but may need some coaching and suggestions to get there.

Before we begin recording his part, I'll give the musician a general idea of how I want him to play it, and will let him hear the original scratch idea created when the song was first written. I might tell the musician:

- "Give me something mean and loud."… or
- "Play the chords soft with distortion."… or
- "Play the part so it sounds like aliens are playing it, etc."

This will put the musician in a certain frame of mind and will open him up creatively. As he plays it down a few times, he will begin to get a better feel for it. Let him play with it a few times before you start giving him too many comments on how to do it better. If you don't give him a chance to get used to it first, he may not be as open to your suggestions later.

If you ever come across a singer or a musician unwilling to try something you ask him to try, phrase your request this way: "Just indulge me, please. I know my idea sounds stupid, but just try it for me one time." Most people will try it for you if you are sincere when you state it like this.

A significant part of being a music producer is knowing how to read a person's personality. It is a lot like being a therapist. You must be flexible and know when to allow a person to act out, or when you need to take control or end the session if you see musicians getting too frustrated or too tired.

A producer must find the best sounds possible. I know that "best sounds" is subjective – there is no right or wrong – but think of yourself as the leader of a safari. It is up to you to explore and find the coolest, most interesting experiences.

For example, if a guitar player brings in a pedal board of effects, I will make sure he tries out many of these to see what cool sounds we come across. I want every musician I bring in to play around with his instrument in as many ways as possible before we record, even if he has to play his instrument upside-down.

I want them to mess around with every button and gadget they bring with them to hear all of the many various sounds they can make. The more sounds they audition for me, the more choices I have in finding the juiciest tones.

CHAPTER 7
DETAILS COUNT

The more music you have listened to throughout your lifetime, the more creative references you have to draw from. If you have heard everything from an African log drum to a Heavy Metal snare drum to percussion from India to Hip-Hop rhythms, then you probably have a good idea what a snare drum should sound like for a given song. The best producers are open to all kinds of music. You may not prefer to listen to a certain type of music personally, but should learn to appreciate it on a creative level.

THE PRODUCER'S ROLE

As a producer, you must think on many different levels:

- Creatively
- Technically
- Administratively

Thinking *creatively* means you should be able to offer ideas, both in charting the overall direction for the project and in the small ideas. An examples of the latter: Do you want the snare drum to ring (resonate), or do you want it to sound flat (sound thuddy or muffled).

Thinking *technically* requires you understand microphones, pre-amps, instruments, signal-flow (how the sound signal moves from one device in the studio to another). If you do not know a lot about the technical side, you can still be an effective music producer, but you will find yourself relying on others (such as the engineer) to make the decisions about specific gear.

Administrative knowledge has to do with understanding paperwork, such as how to do AFM or AFTRA contracts (not as important in these post-modern music industry days), song-split sheets, U.S. Copyright forms, production schedules, project budgets, etc. (Personally, I prefer the creative stuff!)

This chapter is entitled Details Count, but at the same time, do not obsess so much on details that you find yourself losing sight of the big picture. You have to know when to keep the ship sailing and when to pull back and focus on details.

DECISIONS! DECISIONS!

To give you an idea, let's break down a scenario that looks basic enough on the surface, but on second glance, many different choices are revealed.

If we are going to record an electric guitar, we normally will start with the basics:

- Microphone
- Guitar
- Amp
- Musician

Oftentimes, though, the "producer" grabs just about any microphone, puts it up in front of the amp, asks the guitar player to plug in, takes a moment to listen, goes into the control room and then begins recording. Want to know what you get? A mediocre tone (sound coming out of the amp) and an average performance, because the player has not been pushed to give a great performance. So, let's re-examine this whole scenario. As the producer, you must think about:

Microphone

Are we going to use a dynamic mic, a condenser mic, a tube mic, or a ribbon mic on the amp? Are we going to use more than one mic on the amp – a mic directly in front of the speaker and also a room mic to pick up the ambient sounds?

Where should we put the room mic? To answer this, I walk around the room while the guitarist is practicing and find a spot that feels good to my ears. You'll understand if you just try this. We get into mic placement in more detail in the chapter on recording.

> Remember, three important tasks a producer needs to know how to do:
> - Thorough pre-production; in other words, all preparation steps before recording.
> - Get the best performances out of human beings during recording.
> - Identify a compelling sound, whether it be an electric guitar, violin tone, snare drum, vocal tone, etc.

Any additional skills beyond these, such as knowledge of signal flow, professional editing techniques, microphones, outboard gear (e.g., compressors, etc.) will serve to make you a better producer. But understanding the three basic steps puts you ahead of most folks who call themselves a producer.

Particular Instrument Used

Once again, we are faced with many choices. For example: Should we use a double-coil guitar or a single-coil guitar? (Double-coil pickups on a guitar have a beefier, thicker sound when compared to the thinner sound of a single-coil pickup. One is not better than the other, just different.)

Does the instrument stay in tune and/or is it "intonated" well? Does it buzz when plugged in? Should we use the front pickup, middle pickup, or rear pickup? (Each gives a unique tone, the one with the most bass sound toward the front.)

Amp

Are we going for a distorted sound, a clean sound, or something in between? We should play with the bass, mid, and treble knobs on the amp until we find something pleasing.

"How do we know when we have the right settings?" you ask. Well, it is hoped that you will spend some time thinking about the guitar sound during pre-production, before going in to record the guitar for real.

Musician's Touch

I know ten different guitarists who can all play "Stairway to Heaven" really well, but each sounds completely different. A musician's "touch" is the detail we look for in a player. You must be incredibly focused when picking a player; his/her interpretation of what you are going for is important. Some guitarists have a great "fretboard" hand, others have a great "pick" hand, while others have both. A great fretboard hand means the guitarist has outstanding chords where a great pick hand can mean he has superior rhythm patterns. Finding both is even better!

Some players naturally have an aggressive style while others are more laid back. Laid back can mean either he plays behind the beat, or it can mean he does not make contact with the strings very hard.

GETTING A GREAT PERFORMANCE

Even if we have the perfect microphones and the greatest amp ever made, even if the sound coming out makes doves cry, even if the instrument is perfectly tuned, and even if the perfect musician with the right touch for the song is on hand, it won't matter – unless we motivate the player to give us a smashing performance.

This is one of your most important tasks as a producer. You are the first and last line of defense, so it's up to you to make sure what gets recorded is first-rate. At the end of the day, the people who really count – those who will give you your next job – will look at who produced the product. That said, what you lay down on tape had better represent what you are going for.

"How do I know when I have a great performance?" This is a frequently asked question. As a producer, you have to rely on your intuition, that little voice inside you, that gut feeling.

When confronted by some type of stimuli, there are three possible reactions:
- Lifted, excited feeling
- Negative feeling
- Feeling of indifference; neutrality

When you smell something appetizing, like pizza, or see a really cool car, you get that immediate lift. "Wow!" If you witness a car accident, smell a foul odor, or hear fingernails scratching down a chalkboard, you get that downward pull in your gut. If a common car passes you while driving, or if you see an elderly man walk by, you probably get neither a negative nor a positive reaction. This neutral place is how most of us go through our days – relatively uneventful, but with moments of lifts and pulls.

If you pay attention to your gut reactions when listening to a performance you are recording, you will sense, on a small scale, these same feelings. Are you getting any "Oh, man!" impulses? Do you intuitively not like what you are hearing? Or are you not being pulled either way? The goal is to have the "Oh, man!" feelings throughout a performance – or at least here and there.

Don't worry about an instrumentalist or singer getting angry with you when pushing them to do better. At the end of the day, they will thank you for making them dig deeper. We will go further into the performance concept later.

CHAPTER 8
RECORDING BASICS –
GETTING SOUNDS IN

The art of recording music has gone through some huge changes since the year 2000. This was the time when recording in the computer really started to take off.

Before the year 2000, most pros were still recording to two-inch magnetic tape, those huge reels you see in old photos of studios.

Even though computer software has drastically changed how we record music, there are still many techniques that remain the same.

BASICS OF ENGINEERING AND RECORDING

These basic recording principles are:

- **Signal flow:** Moving electricity (sound) from one device to the next, out of one device into the next. (We will get back to this.)
- **Understanding basic recording tools:** Differences between microphones, microphone pre-amps, equalizers, A/D–D/A converters, compressors (more on these later).
- **Microphone placement:** How to mic different instruments, such as drums, guitar amps, vocals, basses, and anything else. (More on this later.)
- **Editing and mixing:** Editing involves cutting, pasting, and altering sounds in your DAW; mixing involves setting the levels so the final product sounds amazing.

HOW DO WE GET MUSIC INTO THE BOX?

Basically, there are three ways to get music into your DAW.

- Record sounds from the real world.
- Record MIDI information.
- Import pre-recorded sounds from a CD/DVD/vinyl or hard-drive.

Recording Sounds from the Real World

These might include voices, guitars, basses, drums, keyboards/pianos, marching bands, DJ turntables, drum machines, thunder – any sound that is created outside of the computer. To record most of these, you need a microphone to turn acoustic sound waves in the air into electrical energy.

A microphone, then, is a transducer that changes air pressure into electricity. On the opposite side, a speaker is a transducer that turns electricity back into acoustic energy. Much more on recording sounds and using microphones later in this chapter!

Recording MIDI Information

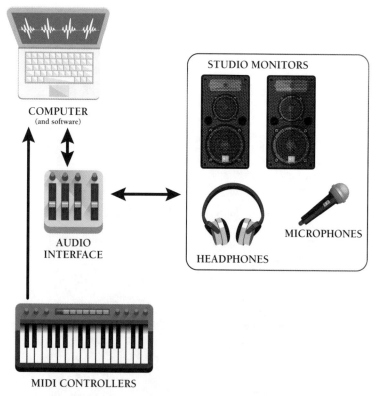

STUDIO MONITORS

COMPUTER
(and software)

AUDIO
INTERFACE

HEADPHONES

MICROPHONES

MIDI CONTROLLERS

What does MIDI stand for? It stands for Musical Instrument Digital Interface. To record MIDI information, you need to hook up a keyboard controller to your computer – one of those mini keyboards.

MIDI might be likened to an old player piano, the kind that plays by itself when you put a paper roll into it. MIDI information would be the equivalent of the holes in the piano roll. Once the paper is punched, it can be put into any piano-roll piano and played. Even though the notes played by the paper roll would be the same from piano to piano, each different piano would give the music an entirely different sound because of each piano's unique tone. The same goes for MIDI. Even though the DAW sequencer records only the pushes of the keys on the keyboard controller, it is the virtual synth (tone generator) you choose in your DAW that creates the actual sound heard. Think of a push of a key on the keyboard controller as firing a bullet, and the virtual instrument as a blanket. The blanket wraps around and adds a coating to the bullet.

Using a MIDI cable, you first need to hook up a keyboard controller to your computer/DAW. Next, you open a virtual synth in your DAW. This computerized synthesizer is where the sounds are generated.

- Keyboard controller: sends a MIDI (trigger) signal to a virtual keyboard in the computer.
- Virtual synthesizer: receives MIDI-trigger note and wraps a sound around it.

Most music software programs have many different synths, each with tons of incredible sounds in them. Before the year 2000, you had to buy synthesizers that cost thousands of dollars each. Getting access to killer keyboard sounds has become so much easier thanks to DAWs.

Importing Pre-recorded Sounds

Importing means to drag a sound already stored on a DVD, CD, or hard drive into your new session, the one you are working on currently. It's kind of like working on a report in the library and going to grab a book off the shelf for some specific info your term paper requires. These books are always available.

In my computer, I have an outstanding library of samples (recorded sounds) ready to be accessed whenever I need them. By "samples," I mean unique sound bites like:

- Crazy vocal phrases
- Lightning and many other nature sounds
- Cool drums and beats
- One-of-a-kind keyboard, bass, and guitar lines
- Car screeches
- Spaceship and laser-beam sounds, and thousands of other bites

Whenever I come across something that catches my ear, whether or not it is musical, I stop and capture the sound and store it on my main hard drive under the heading "sound bank." A money bank is where you store money and a sound bank is where I store cool sound bites onto my hard drive.

Now, all these sounds are available to me whenever I am working on a project. The coolest thing is that my sound bank grows every time I work because I am always stumbling on cool, new sound bites.

GETTING TO KNOW YOUR DAW

There are a many different kinds of DAWs on the market, made by many different companies. The good news is that they all perform the same basic tasks:

- They record sounds.
- They allow you to move the sounds around.
- They allow you to shape the sound using tools like equalizers, reverbs, compressors, and lots of others.
- They allow you to blend all the separate sounds together (final mix) then burn (record) the mix to a CD, DVD, or hard drive.

We could liken all the different DAWs available to all the different types of vehicles at the car dealership. There are plenty to choose from, ranging from luxury to economy, but they all do the same basic things:

- Drive
- Turn left or right
- Stop
- Back up

If you know the gas pedal, brake pedal, and steering wheel, you can drive pretty much any vehicle, whether it's a go-kart or an 18-wheeler. The same goes for DAWs. If you understand the basics of:

- Recording: Getting sounds in the box.
- Editing: Moving sounds around, if necessary.
- Playback: Listening to what was captured and altered.

…then you can pretty much sit down in front of any DAW and understand it without too much difficulty. You simply have to make yourself familiar with where the tools (gas pedal, brake pedal, steering wheel) are located in each different DAW.

If your goal is to operate gear and be an engineer – something I did for 15 years before the advent of the DAW – then you might want to learn a few different DAWs so you can work with many different clients.

If you want to produce your own music, you might wish to focus on one or two different DAWs and get really good at one of them so the technology and tools don't slow your creative process. There is nothing worse than having a promising idea for a song in your head and being unable to express it because you can't handle the digital equipment the way it needs to be handled.

But when you understand the technology like the back of your hand, you don't even have to think about that aspect. You can focus solely on getting what's in your head into the box exactly as you hear it. This is the difference between just laying your stuff down and truly crafting something.

CHAPTER 9
HARDWARE

In this chapter, we'll look at the basics, giving attention to some of the most commonly used recording gear:

- Microphones
- DAW Interfaces
- Equalizers
- Compressors

MICROPHONES

To keep it simple, let's categorize mics into four groups:

- Dynamic mics
- Condenser mics
- Tube mics
- Ribbon mics

Dynamic Mics

Sennheiser 421   *AKG D112*   *Shure SM57*

Think of these types of microphones as unpowered mics. Dynamic mics have no electricity running through them, unlike condenser mics and tube mics. A dynamic (unpowered) mic is like a windmill. A windmill needs lots of wind to make the rotor blades move. A small breeze won't do. Likewise, a dynamic mic will not pick up a sound unless the sound is aimed right into the mic. If a dynamic mic is not right up on the source of the sound (voice, guitar, amp, etc.), it will pick up only a tiny bit of the sound.

Also, dynamic mics can take lots of sound volume without getting damaged, so you can put it right up against a guitar amp with the volume set on 10 and it will work just fine. This is not the case with condenser mics and tube mics. Since they utilize electricity, they are much more sensitive and will get damaged if you put them right up against a loud guitar amp speaker.

Dynamic mics are really good for "isolation" purposes, too. What does that mean? If you are miking a drum kit, you would probably use dynamic mics on the close drums for two reasons:

- The mics can handle the loud volume of the drums.
- Each mic will pick up only the drum it is aimed at. This way, you can record the snare, toms, hi-hat, and kick at the same time.

Condenser Mics

AKG 414   AKG 451   Neumann U87

Unlike dynamic mics, condenser mics do have electricity running through them when in use. This power running through the mics makes them much more sensitive than an unpowered/dynamic mic.

Using the windmill example from earlier, imagine the big blades have a small motor attached to the shaft to help even soft breezes turn the blades. This way, even the lightest breeze would move the rotor blades on the windmill. It's sort of like a car with power steering, where a small motor assists you in turning the heavy front wheels of the car. The same is true with condenser mics; they pick up the faintest of sounds.

The name of the type of electricity that runs through condenser mics is called *phantom power* or *48 volts*. All microphone pre-amps generate phantom power. (We will discuss mic pre-amps in detail in the next section.) When you connect a condenser mic to a mic pre-amp using a microphone cord, electricity travels two ways through the mic cord:

- Mic-pre sends phantom power to the mic
- Mic sends sound to the mic-pre

When you use a dynamic (unpowered) mic, the signal goes only from the mic to the mic-pre. Remember, dynamic mics don't require phantom power. Every mic-pre has a phantom power on/off switch. When using a dynamic mic, you leave phantom power *off*.

Let's compare what we've said about dynamic and condenser mics so far:

DYNAMIC MICS
- Less sensitive to soft sounds.
- Handle very loud sounds.
- Pick up only what is right in front of them, so they are better for isolating sound.
- Unpowered mic: Only the wind from your voice or instrument makes mechanism move inside the mic.
- Use on: Snare drum, inside kick drum, up close on guitar amp screen, vocal mic onstage for live performance, etc.
- Costs: approximately $35–$200.
- Popular models: Shure SM-57, Shure SM-58 AKG D-112 (good for bass amps and kick drums), Sennheiser 421.

CONDENSER MICS
- More sensitive to soft sounds.
- Do not handle very loud sounds well close up.
- Pick up anything and everything in the area. Since they are more sensitive, they sound cleaner and clearer than dynamic mics. Not good for isolating sound, though.
- Use electricity called phantom power to make the mic more sensitive. Even the softest sound will be picked up.
- Good for recording vocals in an isolated, soundproof room – use as a room mic to record drum kit, acoustic guitar, piano, the sound of an audience, etc.
- Costs: $100–$3,000 and up. (You can get a good-sounding condenser mic now for a few hundred dollars.)
- Popular models: Neumann U-87, AKG 414, AKG 451, Blue Bluebird, MXL-V67g. There are plenty on the market these days.

Before we move on and talk about tube mics, let's discuss a couple of things that all microphones have in common.

- Pick-up patterns
- Diaphragm sizes

Pick-up Patterns

The area of the room a mic will record is called the *pick-up pattern*. There are three basic types:

- Cardioid
- Omni
- Figure 8

cardioid mic

A cardioid mic picks up sounds in front of the mic only. Its name based on the root word "cardiac," which refers to the heart.

Imagine a Valentine heart. If the mic is put at the point of the heart shape where the opposing arches meet in the center to form a V, the area inside the heart shape is what the mic will pick up best. Anything outside the heart shape will not be picked up quite so well. This is the most common position in which to set the mic, because you usually want to pick up only what is in front of the microphone.

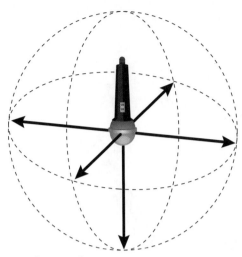

omnidirectional mic

Omnidirectional means the mic will pick up anything from any angle. It is represented as a circle. For instance, if you have ten people to record at one time, you could set the mic to this pick-up pattern, then ask them to form a circle with their shoulders touching. The mic is placed directly in the center. All ten singers would be picked up by the mic equally.

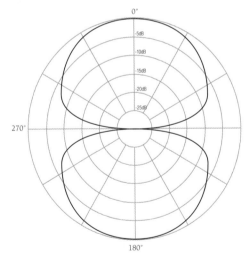

Figure 8 mic

Figure 8 indicates that the mic will pick up in the shape of the number eight. If you were to place a mic right where the circles meet in the middle, the area inside each circle is what would be most picked up by setting the mic to this pattern.

Let's say you have two actors reading dialogue who need to look at each other as they record their parts. Hypothetically, you would position them facing each other with the mic directly between them. The only problem with this scenario is that both actors will be recorded to the same track, but this example gives you an idea of what Figure 8 is.

Diaphragm Size

A diaphragm is the filament that moves in the mic when sound pressure pushes against it. Microphone diaphragms range between three sizes: large, regular, and small.

Large diaphragm   *Regular diaphragm*   *Small diaphragm (or "pencil")*

Why would we use one diaphragm size over another? To answer this, we need to understand sound waves a bit. We can classify sound into three groups:

- Treble (high end)
- Mid-range
- Bass (low end)

Think of sound waves traveling through the air just like ripples moving through water. Imagine the up-and-down curved shape of a water wave.

If you drop a pebble in a pond of still water, you will see the waves begin to radiate out from where the pebble hits the water. This is how sound waves travel through the air. If the waves are closer together as they radiate out, your ear will be tickled faster and you will hear a sizzling, high-pitched sound. On the other hand, if the waves are farther apart from one another, your ear will perceive it as a muffled, bass-y sound. Take a moment and visualize these images in your mind.

So, we can conclude that bass waves are "wider" than trebly, high-end sounds that have waves traveling much closer together. By wider, we mean there is more empty space between each wave. The waves are reaching your ear less frequently – or at a lower frequency. Aha!

Back to the diaphragm size – the bigger the diaphragm, the more bass the mic will pick up. The smaller the diaphragm, the more treble, or high-end, it will pick up.

High-end sounds like sizzle, mid-range sounds like an announcer on a loudspeaker at a stadium – very nasal. Low-end sounds like your reaction when you taste something delicious and say "Mmm" to yourself. So, sizzle, nasal, and "Mmm" all work together to make up something that sounds like everyday life. As an engineer, you need be able to hear each of these general tones in everything you listen to.

To sum up diaphragm size: Use a large diaphragm mic to pick up a bass amp or a kick drum. Use a pencil microphone to pick up something with lots of sizzle and shimmer – like an acoustic guitar being strummed or cymbals on a drum set.

Generally speaking, many dynamic (unpowered) mics have regular/mid-sized diaphragms. Condenser mics usually have either large, regular, or pencil diaphragms.

Tube Mics

Neumann U47 tube mic

AKG P820 tube mic

Like condenser mics, tube mics are powered with electricity. But unlike condenser mics, tube mics do not use phantom power. They have their own electricity generator.

Each individual tube mic has its own "power supply" box. It's kind of like the mic brings its lunch to the studio, as opposed to condenser mics being stuck with eating the cafeteria food, which is generic phantom power.

Both tube mics and condenser mics are very sensitive, much more so than dynamic mics. They pick up more high-end sizzle and low-end "Mmm" than dynamic mics. You could say condenser mics and tube mics sound better than dynamic mics, but the latter are better for isolating sound and can take lots more volume than tubes and condensers.

So why would you use a tube mic instead of a condenser mic or vice versa? Well, tube mics are usually a little more delicate than condenser mics, which means a condenser can take a bit more volume than a tube mic. But the real difference is in the tone, the character, of each.

As an example: If I were to throw up a handful of sand between you and me, as the sand fell between us, I'd still be able to see you through the falling sand. The dense sand represents the tone of a condenser mic.

Next, I throw up some baby powder between us and as it falls I can see you. But unlike the sand, the baby powder is more transparent than the sand. It has a more mist-like quality.

So, you could say that a tube mic has a more transparent sound – as if you can see through the sound – as opposed to a condenser mic, which has a denser sound, kind of like you can actually touch it.

CONDENSER MIC
- Use on each instrument in an orchestra.
- Record a rapper who has a strong voice.
- Place six feet away from guitar amp.

TUBE MIC
- Record an orchestra from the audience.
- Record Celine Dion, who has a silky voice.
- Place across the room from a guitar amp to pick up the overall room sound.

Ribbon Mics

Ribbon microphones were an early microphone design. The first ones were invented in the early 1920s. They were a catalyst in the evolution of the audio recording process due to their ability to capture a wide range of frequencies and to produce a warm, close-to-full-range sound.

Remember, at the turn of the 1900s, singing into a microphone that looked like an orange traffic cone was considered standard practice, so the ribbon mic was a huge step forward.

Ribbon mics became less popular as modern, more durable dynamic and condenser mics evolved. Ribbon mics were much more fragile than the newer dynamic and condenser mics that were hitting the market through the 1950s forward. As the 1960s evolved, along with the so-called British Invasion of music of this time (The Beatles, Rolling Stones, et al.), sound-reinforcement systems (public-address systems) became more and more popular as more rock concerts were held.

Rock concerts relied on microphones that were both roadworthy and able to handle very loud volumes, such as miking electric guitar amplifiers onstage and projecting them to 100,000 fans via the P. A. system. An old-school ribbon mic would have gotten its socks blown off.

Recently, though, ribbon mics have made a comeback by cool companies like Royer Mics who have updated the old ribbon design and are making new, modern hot-rod ribbon mics every bit as durable both construction-wise and sound-pressure-wise as any dynamic mic. Royer's flagship ribbon microphone is the R-121 Studio Ribbon mic. It has become the go-to mic for many producers and engineers for capturing great guitar-amp tones or anything with a ton of volume.

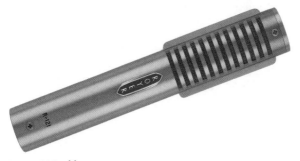

Royer 121 ribbon mic

Generally speaking, traditional ribbon mics are usually known for their lo-fi, round, warm tone. They usually have a much smoother high-end than typical dynamic mics. Another popular ribbon mic is the Coles 4038 model.

Coles 4038 ribbon mic

I really like using these Coles 4038s as ambient room mics when recording drums. They lend a John Bonham/Led Zeppelin drum tone where the drums sound as if they were recorded in a castle, which Zeppelin's were at times. They produce a dark, smooth, warm, compressed sound.

Lastly, like dynamic mics, ribbon mics are unpowered mics, which means they do not use phantom power like a condenser mic, or require any type of power supply like a tube mic. Only the "wind" from the sound source makes the thin strip of metallic material (ribbon) vibrate. This thin strip is surrounded by a magnetic field (opposing poles of a fixed magnet), so that when the ribbon flutters and sloshes back and forth across this placid magnetic field, the disruption creates a signal that is then amplified by the mic pre-amp.

Accidentally running phantom power to a vintage ribbon mic could damage the fragile ribbon, but modern ribbon mics are usually not affected by phantom power if turned on by mistake. Another common feature of most ribbon mics is that they have a figure-eight pickup pattern only, meaning they pick up equally well on both sides of the mic. This makes ribbon mics great candidates for applying the classic X-Y (also known as a Blumlein Pair) miking technique.

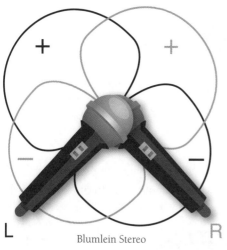

L   Blumlein Stereo   R

Blumlein Pair diagram

Microphone Pre-amp

API pre-amp

Neve pre-amp

A microphone always plugs into a mic pre-amp. A pre-amp is simply an amplifier, just like a guitar plugs into a guitar amplifier. Mic pre-amps come in many shapes and colors and are made by many different companies, but they all do the same thing: pump up the level of the microphone so the signal can be used and manipulated in your session. A microphone generates just a tiny amount of signal on its own.

Think of a washer – you know, looks like a flat, metal donut and is used to fasten a screw. Let's say the washer is magnetized. So now we have a washer that is a magnet. Now imagine the space in the middle of the washer – if the washer is a magnet, you can imagine an invisible magnetic field in the hole of the washer, kind of like a thin sheet of magnetism reaching across the empty space.

Take a thin nail and put its tip right in the middle of the hole of the washer, not touching any of the sides of the washer. The tip of the nail is dipping its toe in the middle of our magnetic lake. If there is no activity, the tip of the nail will sit there and be pulled evenly by all the sides of the magnetic washer. Everything is just chillin'.

But let's say I put my mouth close to the nail tip and yell. The vibration from my voice will make the tip of the nail vibrate just a little bit. When this happens, the nail that is suspended in this invisible lake of magnetism across the washer's hole creates a disruption in the calm magnetic field, kind of like sloshing a stick back and forth in water. This slight disruption creates a blip of electromagnetic energy and is sent to the mic-pre amplifier through the mic cable.

So, now you can imagine how tiny of a signal is generated by the nail tip vibrating in the magnetic field of the tiny washer. This is where the mic-pre comes in. The mic-pre receives this tiny signal and amplifies it. Think of an uninflated balloon. It is only so big, but when you blow up the balloon, it becomes 20 times its uninflated size.

Most of the mass of the inflated balloon is the air blown inside and only the outer shell is the balloon itself. I make this analogy to illustrate the importance of the mic-pre, which is this: It "inflates" the tiny signal from the microphone with electricity. The original signal is like the outer shell of the balloon, but the majority of the size is the electricity the mic-pre has pumped into the tiny signal.

The moral of the story: The better the quality of the mic-pre, the better the electricity you are using to puff up the signal. The better the electricity, the better the sound. It is that simple. The mic-pre is one of the most important pieces in the studio.

DAW INTERFACES

DAW stands for Digital Audio Workstation. There are many different DAWs currently available on the market. Several examples are:

- Pro Tools
- Reason
- Logic
- Ableton
- PreSonus Studio One

- Cubase
- GarageBand
- Digital Performer
- FL Studio
- et al.

To clarify, DAWs come in two parts:
- Software
- Hardware

Software: What you see on the screen.

Hardware: The physical piece of gear that works with the software. It is what you actually plug the microphone or instrument into. It also allows you to control the volume of the speakers and headphones.

This piece of hardware is also called the interface. Interface units commonly contain different components, listed below.

A/D–D/A CONVERTER

A = analog; D = digital. So, analog to digital and digital to analog. To explain, when you speak into a microphone, the signal generated by the mic is in analog form, meaning it is analogous – or the "same" as the original. But to get it into the DAW, the signal must be converted from analog into digital form.

The A/D converter in your interface basically takes pictures of the analog signal and converts it into a series of snapshots represented as cluster-combinations of ones and zeros. Now, these digital snapshots are fed into the DAW.

Once inside the DAW, you can manipulate the sound however you choose. But then in order to hear what you are chopping up on the screen, the digital signal must be converted from digital back to analog so it can be fed to the speakers and heard.

So really, sounds are fed from the real world into the A/D converter, which allows the converted signal to be fed into the DAW. Fractions of a second later, the sound is converted back from digital to analog so we can hear what we just did. There sure is a lot going on in thousandths of a second.

This slight gap can cause what is called "latency." DAWs allow you to adjust how big or small this gap can be. Obviously, if you are recording a guitar part and you can feel and hear a slight delay between when you strike the strings and when you hear it in your headphones, you have too much latency; it will usually impair your performance. At this point, go in and shorten the gap so no delay is heard and you can lay down a great performance without the distraction of the gap. But by narrowing the gap, you are sucking lots of computer horsepower, so if you have lots of tracks already recorded with tons of effects engaged on tracks, shortening your latency gap usually makes your computer slow way down and possibly even crash repeatedly. Thus, it is a constant balancing act of managing computer processing resources. If you are a beginner at using your DAW, don't trip on this if you are not aware of it. Your DAW is defaulted to a setting that will balance out pretty well. As you feel more comfortable with your gear and begin to create bigger sessions with more and more tracks, adjusting latency values will be a natural progression for you to absorb.

MIC-PRE(S)

Another piece of gear in the interface is a mic-pre, or multiple mic-pres. The number of mic-pres in the interface is what determines how many mics you can record at the same time. If you need to use four mics on a drum set but have two microphone inputs (mic-pres) on your interface, guess what… you are limited to only two mics.

Many times, an engineer/producer may want to use a better quality mic-pre than is supplied by the interface. In the past, mic-pres that came with interfaces were usually of basic quality – not bad, but not the best. For that reason, engineers often choose to plug the microphone into a totally separate, better quality mic-pre, then send that signal to the interface to be converted from analog to digital by the A/D converter in the interface. By doing this, we are bypassing the inferior mic-pre in the interface and only utilizing the A/D converter in the interface.

SPEAKER VOLUME/HEADPHONE VOLUME AND JACK

The interface also allows you to hook speakers up to it and has a headphone jack with a separate volume control. So you can really see that the interface of a DAW is like the dashboard of a car. It allows you to interact with the system; it is the magic mirror between the real world and the digital world inside the computer.

EQUALIZERS

Equalizers are probably the most commonly used "cosmetic" devices. By cosmetic, we mean the ability to change the shade or "color" of any sound. An equalizer (EQ) is the equivalent of a make-up artist's case of lipsticks, skin toners, eyeliners, etc. Of the main tools of the trade – mic-pres, compressors, EQs – the EQ is the one that usually makes the most obvious changes to a sound.

Side Discussion – Frequency

Think of frequency this way: The higher the frequency, the higher the pitch of a note and the higher the sizzle of a sound and vice versa. To go into it a bit more, we need to have a basic understanding of how sound travels through the air and how we perceive sound.

We humans are "swimming" through air molecules, just like a fish swimming through water. Water molecules are touching and pressing on every part of the fish. Air molecules are touching and pressing on every part of us.

Those multi-colored ball-pits at kids' indoor playgrounds are also a good representation. When a kid jumps into a pit, the balls below his butt get pushed out of the way, which in turn bump into the balls next to them, which then bump into the balls next to these, and so on and so on.

The balls don't necessarily move. The energy is transferred from one ball to the next, kind of like that toy you might see sitting on an executive's desk where five or six small metal balls are hanging from what looks like fishing line; as you pull the ball on the end and let it go, it hits the second ball, but then the last ball swings out on the opposite side. The energy is transferred through the middle balls, which stay stationary.

So, when someone claps his hands, the air molecules between his hands get pushed aside, which bump into the neighboring air molecules and so on all the way until the air molecules resting against your eardrums get pushed. These then push against your eardrums, which then tickle nerve mechanisms inside your brain. So, to sum it all up, your eardrums get pushed, which the brain picks up and then chemically interprets as sound. Your world is coming apart as you read this. (Laugh.) Is sound really sound, or just brain chemicals interpreting changes in air pressure? Creepy!

Sound is invisible, but there is a way to show it visually: This is done by what is called a "waveform." We have all seen waveforms, the squiggly, colorful patterns on the computer screen.

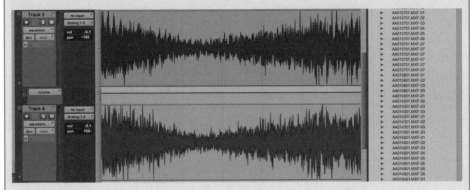

There are two basic ways of measuring sound, amplitude and frequency.

- Amplitude is how tall any point of the waveform is at any given spot. The taller, the louder.
- Frequency is how many times the wave completes a cycle in one second.

Imagine this: You're in a pond of water with your body completely submerged and only your head poking out. The water is right at eye level, with your nose and mouth just underneath the water surface, eyes above. While you are eye level in the water, a small rock drops into the pond and starts a wave. You see the wave as both slightly above the water's surface, then slightly below the water's surface. This is how a wave moves through water.

So, the water is not the wave and the wave is not the water. The wave passes through and disrupts the water. The wave and the water are two separate things altogether. The wave is really invisible.

Hertz is a way of measuring the frequency (pitch or tone) of a sound. Stay with me here:

1 hertz (1Hz) is equal to one cycle per second.
(What the heck does this mean?)

It is a way of measuring sound. Think back to being eye level with the water in the pond. A "cycle" means one up-stroke and one downstroke of the water wave.

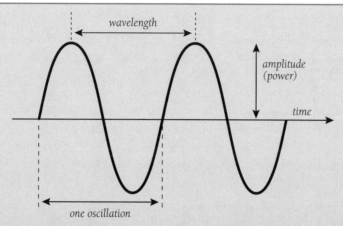

one oscillation

So, if three cycles pass a given point in one second, that would be known as 3Hz. In the same way, 50Hz would be 50 cycles (up and down waves) moving past a given point in one second.

The letter "k" is often used to mean 1,000. With that in mind, 3kHz = 3,000 hertz.

Don't get caught up in trying to analyze this too much. Think of it this way: The higher the *hertz*, the higher the pitch. If referring to equalization (EQ), the higher the hertz, the higher the tone, or "sizzle."

Remember:

High-end	Treble	sizzle
8kHz to 20kHz		e.g., cymbals; saying the letter S
Mid-range	Mids	nasal
900Hz to 8kHz		e.g., announcer at a stadium; saying "Ah"
Low-end	Bass	muffled
20Hz to 900Hz		e.g., saying "Umm"

Human hearing ranges anywhere from 20Hz (low end) to 20kHz (high end). Obviously, some people don't hear as high as 20kHz where others may hear higher than 20k. Dogs hear past 20kHz, much closer to 45kHz.

Think of hertz this way: 2,500 Hz (2.5kHz) means your eardrum flaps 2,500 times in one second. There you go! Easy to visualize!

Okay, back to equalization (EQ)…

There are two types of equalizers common to engineering:
- Parametric
- Graphic

Parametric

Graphic

A *parametric EQ* allows you to scroll through many different frequencies, whereas a *graphic EQ* has pre-set frequencies. Parametric refers to allowing the separate control of various "parameters" on the unit.

> **Another Measurement of Sound: 1 dB = 1 Decibel**
> To give you an idea, the difference between the loudness of snapping your finger and clapping is approximately 5dB. So you really can't hear the difference between something that is 50dB and 51dB. At the end of the day, you'll turn a knob until it sounds good to you, and that's all that matters.

Let's return to our discussion of EQ. First of all, an EQ allows the user to either increase or take away whatever frequencies he chooses. To make it even simpler, let's break down what frequencies sound like by putting them into three categories:
- Highs
- Mids
- Lows

Sonic Phonics

- Highs sound like sizzle or "sss."
- Mids sound like someone talking through a bullhorn ("ahh").
- Lows sound as if someone were saying "mmm."

These three tones (sss, ahh, or mmm) make up what we hear as full-range sound/ high-fidelity. These "sonic phonics" are our highs, mids, and lows. You combine: **pitch** (frequency; high notes, low notes) with **volume** (amplitude) and **tone** (sss, ahh, mmm) and you begin to create unique sounds.

I can hear someone asking, "Why and when would I need to EQ a sound anyway?" The question is answered using a comparative question: "When and/or why would I need to salt and pepper my food?"

The answer is obvious. When the food is bland or not flavorful enough for us, we spice it up. This question/answer is as varied as there are individuals. Everyone is going to taste their food differently.

We instinctively know whether or not we like the taste of something – much more clearly than whether or not we like the sound of something. This means we must train our ears more. How do we do that? A good way is to listen to as much music as we can, to expose ourselves to as much music as possible.

It is equally important to listen to as many different types of music as possible, from Classical to Metal to Electronica to Country. Listen to everything from Hip-Hop and Bluegrass to Mariachi and African tribal. This is the best way to condition one's ear. The more music one is exposed to, the more references one has to draw from when faced with a particular sound. It is that simple.

EQing is as subjective and personal as beauty is. It is totally up to you. Another useful way to help you know whether or not you should EQ is to reference your sound to a similar one from something you like. If a snare you are recording is not making you smile when you hear it, but you don't know what is bothering you about it, play a song that you like that is somewhat similar to what you are working on; analyze what theirs sounds like. This makes it much easier.

Even if you are just initially constructing/crafting the drums for your song, you can reference a song by an artist you like and focus on the sound of their snare drum, for instance. Listen to how it sounds. Is it high-pitched or deep and thuddy? Is it loud in the overall mix of the song or buried under the other instruments? Is it dry (no reverb) or wet (sounds like it is played in a stadium)? Analyzing the snare this way will give you a great reference as to where you may or may not want to take your snare sound. This can help to shape the overall production direction for the song.

Practice EQing: Whether you are EQing a single hi-hat, a cluster of background vocals at one time, or EQing an entire mix, practice against a reference in your spare time. Go back and forth between something out there you like, and what you are working on. Try and make yours sound like the reference. This is great practice.

There are really two steps when EQing:
- Find the frequency you want to add or lessen.
- Add the frequency or lessen it.

With a parametric EQ, we have many more options in terms of the specific frequencies we can play with.
- First, we dial the frequency selector to whatever frequency we want to play with.
- Then we turn the gain/reduce knob to add or lessen that frequency.

Generally speaking, parametric EQs are used in the recording studio and graphic EQs are many times used in live settings for shaping the overall sound of the P. A. system.

Each night, a band plays a different arena and each arena sounds different due to whether the walls are concrete or carpeted, etc. There are countless factors that can differentiate one room from another. So, the sound guy can use a graphic EQ and "shape" the room with the sliders. If the room has too much mid-range or brightness, he can contour the room accordingly. By lowering the sliders on the right side of the graphic EQ below the neutral-middle (zero) position, the soundman is decreasing the treble of what is coming out of the P. A. system, thus compensating for the mid-range/bright sound of the room itself. The left side of the graphic EQ are the low-end frequencies, and high-end frequencies are on the right side.

A graphic EQ is good for overall, general shaping, as opposed to a parametric, which is better for specific shaping – like operating with a laser beam.

The Magic Frequencies

There are certain frequencies that work well on all types of sounds – from kick drums to guitars to vocals to snare drums to violins, etc. I call these the Magic Frequencies:
- Add   2dB of 10kHz   adds sizzle air
- Add   1dB of 6kHz   adds definition/diction
- Add   1dB of 2kHz   attack/presence
- Reduce   2dB of 200Hz   takes out muddiness
- Add   2dB of 110Hz   clean, low end

If these frequencies are applied to whatever sound accordingly, it will take on a more defined shape. Let's describe each of these frequencies.
- **10k:** This is like applying a bit of lip gloss. A little lip gloss makes a marked improvement in appearance. So, 10k adds a little shine, a little sparkle to every sound.
- **6k:** Adds definition to any sound; adds increased diction to any vocal performance. A little 6k will make a mumbling rapper sound like he's Laurence Olivier reciting Shakespeare. 6kHz is like defining the eyes of a face. A person's character is usually defined by the eyes.

- **2k:** This is where the "attack" resides. 2k is that sound of the stick making contact with the snare drum; the sound of the beater of the kick drum making contact with the kick drum head. It is that "pointy" sound. Add a tad and you will enhance the presence of any sound.

  By the same token, 2kHz can be an annoyance and needs to be reduced from some sounds. The Jerry Lewis alter ego or maybe the actress Fran Drescher could be considered to have that whiny kind of voice. Heavy metal guitars as well have a tendency to be very mid-rangy at times. Rolling out a few decibels of 2kHz will usually clean them up a bit, so that they are not so annoying.

- **200Hz–500Hz:** These frequencies tend to sound really "muddy." I usually get great results by rolling off a few decibels of 200Hz or 250 from just about everything. It truly opens up most sounds. Think of the frequencies between 200–500Hz as kind of like a beer belly. It is not really attractive on anyone.

  The only time I may add 200Hz to an instrument might be if a tom-tom is missing the "bounce" of the "doooom" sound characteristic to them. This is the only time when these frequencies seem to help.

- **90–130Hz:** This frequency range is really clean, open low-end. Like a great butt, it is round in just the right places and invisible in just the right places. What more can I say?

Hardware vs. Plug-ins

I am asked all the time whether using a compressor that is bolted into a rack is better than its virtual counterparts or vice versa. This is a great question. Before giving an answer, let's explore how this came to be.

Virtual LA-2A Compressor

Real LA-2A Compressor

Obviously, there were no virtual compressors, EQs, or anything else before (let's say) the mid-1990s. Recording equipment in the "olden days" looked something like this:

Going back even further, audio recording began to evolve in sophistication around the 1940s or so. Compressors and EQs were all hard devices. Not until DAWs (digital audio workstations such as Pro Tools, Reason, et al.) did virtual versions of compressors, EQs, reverbs, etc. appear. When virtual plug-ins first began to come out, there were not a lot to choose from. Some were quite good and some were not. Software makers such as the effects-plug-ins companies Waves and Bomb Factory, among others, were pioneers in creating virtual versions of classic "hard" devices. Nowadays there are many companies and an abundance of virtual plug-ins available.

Whether a particular hard device or its virtual counterpart is better is a subjective answer. Both have their pros and cons. The hard devices become more idiosyncratic as they age. Years of wear and tear makes gear perform differently. Some studios will endure heavy cigarette smoke, others heavy weed smoke. Some gear has had liquid spilled on it, while others have been dropped on the ground by accident.

An LA-2A compressor in one studio will more than likely have a different sound/ feel than an identical LA-2A in a different studio. So when you find a really sweet-sounding one, you get spoiled. You go to another room and it is not as sweet; it sounds much more brittle.

On the other hand, virtual plug-ins always stay consistent from one computer to another; an LA-2A on one computer will sound exactly like an LA-2A on another rig. Also, the virtual devices will recall exactly the same settings you had every time you open the session, as opposed to a hard unit that will always be just a little off, even in the best scenario.

Virtual outboard gear (plug-ins) also can be made to "glitch out" on purpose. By "over-tweaking" the controls on some virtual devices, the gear will do things the authors of the software had never intended. One popular example of this is the "Antares AutoTune syndrome." The "robotic" sound is actually the device freaking out and over-processing. But, serendipitously, it sounds unique. An early popular example of this was heard on Cher's '90s hit, "Do You Believe in Love After Love?" Artist T-Pain then wore the auto-tune sound into the ground during the mid-2000s.

In conclusion, hard devices tend to have individual personality while virtual versions have uniformity and the ability to be "glitched-out."

COMPRESSORS

Compressors are curious devices, probably the most misunderstood devices in a studio.

Nowadays we have plug-ins, virtual effect boxes of every kind in every DAW (digital audio work station). Plug-ins are much easier to use than their real-world counterparts – actual, physical compressors, reverbs, etc. – found in racks at studios. This is because most of them are positioned to a default setting so that when you first mount the plug-in to a channel in your system, the plug-in pretty much does what it is intended to do. This is especially true of utility devices like compressors.

What I aim to do first in this discussion of compressors is give the user a firm understanding of what compressors and limiters are typically used for, what the basic knobs do on a compressor, and then – most importantly – how to apply a compressor to your life and music and make people's heads nod up and down. Without practical application, it's all just a bunch of theoretical rhetoric.

To begin, let's make a distinction between a compressor and a limiter. Think of a compressor as a lazy limiter, or a limiter as a compressor on steroids. More on this later.

To keep it simple, first ask yourself, "Do I want to protect a sound or destroy a sound?" "What?" I can hear people saying, "Protect or destroy?" A sound we might want to "protect" could possibly be a vocal, and a sound we may want to "destroy" or "obliterate" might be a snare drum sound.

Look at a door near you, any door. If you were to throw a piece of fruit at the door, you would hear a "pop" as the fruit smashed into the door. Think of this as destroying a sound.

Now, imagine you had the power to turn the door into a wall of cotton balls. If you were to throw another piece of fruit at this soft wall, when the fruit hit the wall of cotton balls, it would sink into the wall and then drop softly to the floor, unsmashed and fully intact. The wall of cotton balls would protect the fruit instead of demolishing it the way the hard surface did.

From these examples, if we were about to record a drum set and the snare drum does not have the "pop" we want, we can insert a compressor between the microphone and the recorder – actually between the mic-pre and the recorder – so that the snare collides as if into a brick wall and gets splattered by the compressor. It will create more of a "pop," similar to the fruit thrown at a door.

At the other end of the spectrum, if we are about to record a lead vocal, we don't want the vocal to distort by arriving at the recording device at too hot a level. In order to prevent this potential distortion, we again place a compressor between the mic-pre and the recorder and set the compressor so that it acts like a wall of cotton balls protecting the vocal from "hurting its head." Think of a gymnast on a trampoline jumping so high that she hits her head on the ceiling above.

These are just two basic examples. Obviously, in the real world there is an infinite number of possible scenarios. We are discussing two opposing scenarios to show the extreme contrast and wide range of possible uses of compressors.

Next, let's discuss how to turn a compressor into either a "hard" surface or "soft" surface. There are two controls commonly found on most compressors:
- Threshold
- Ratio/Compression

Threshold dial (L); Ratio/Compression dial (R)

To understand what these knobs do, let's again use an analogy. Let's think of a racquetball court. It has a ceiling that is part of the court, so if the ball hits the ceiling, the ball is still in play.

Now imagine there is a huge cranking lever just outside the court where we can raise the height of the ceiling 30 feet into the air or lower the ceiling so low that we would have to play racquetball on our knees. We can raise or lower the ceiling either up or down. This is "threshold." Stay with me here, there's more to come.

Side Discussion – Threshold

We live in a world where we turn knobs from left to right to get more volume, left to right to get more heat, left to right to get more water, etc. The crazy thing about the threshold knob is that it is backward. One would think that when you turn the threshold "up" (to the right), you are adding more of it to the sound. This is not true; you turn the threshold knob from right to left to add more. Let's explore.

Think of the threshold knob again as being able to either raise or lower the ceiling of a racquetball court. If the knob is on "10," all the way to the right, then the ceiling of the racquetball court is on the tenth floor, as opposed to the knob's being on "1," which would mean that the ceiling is on the first floor. If the ceiling were on the first floor, there would be a bigger chance that the ball would hit the ceiling, as compared to it's being on the tenth floor where the ceiling would be much higher.

If the ceiling is really high, the ball (representing the sound) will not hit the ceiling as much as it would if it were low. Therefore, the higher the threshold, the less the ball is affected by the ceiling.

Threshold is only half of the equation. Let's now talk about the other common knob on the compressor, ratio/compression.

Ratio/Compression

The "ratio" knob is sometimes labeled "compression" and vice versa. In essence, they mean the same thing. To make another simple analogy: If the threshold knob controls how high or low the ceiling of the racquetball court is, the ratio/compression knob controls what the ceiling is made of.

We can choose to make it as soft as a ceiling of cotton balls, or as hard as steel. Think of it this way: the lower the ratio, the softer the ceiling. (Compressor/ratio-knobs allow you to choose from 1:1 and on up, as opposed to the ratio knob on a limiter, which starts at 10:1 or 20:1 and goes up).

- 1:1 Cotton balls
- 2:1 Pillows
- 3:1 Rubber (good default setting to start at; Goldilocks setting: not too hard, not too soft)
- 4:1 Cardboard
- 5:1 Balsa wood/Styrofoam
- 6:1 Wood
- 7:1 Concrete, etc.

To sum things up about compressors, here is a simple way to go about applying them:

1. See if there are any sounds in your production that need either more "pop," or need to be "softened up." For example, a snare drum often needs more pop, and a vocal often needs to be softened up, especially if the singer gets really loud during certain parts of the song.
2. Insert the compressor of your choice on the track/sound you want to either smash or soften up.
3. Immediately set the ratio to 3:1, and turn the threshold knob all the way up to the right (if it is a knob), or all the way up (if a vertical slider). A 3:1 ratio is a good medium-strength ceiling hardness to start at. Not too hard, not too soft.
4. Next, put the track with the compressor on it in "solo" mode so you will be able to hear how you are affecting the sound.
5. Now, begin to lower the threshold slider or knob slowly until you see the GR (gain reduction) light/meter begin to blink. When this happens, it means you have lowered the ceiling of our imaginary gym down to where the gymnast's head is touching the ceiling each time she jumps up. I call this the "point of intersection."
6. From here, use your ears. What do you want to achieve? Do you want to smash the sound? If so, lower the threshold until you like what you hear.

If you want to protect a vocal sound from spiking too high, back the ratio down to 2:1, and lower the threshold just a little bit to keep the loud notes from hitting their head too hard on the ceiling.

There is no right or wrong way to use a compressor. As long as you have an idea of what it can do, it is up to you to be creative with it and make it do whatever you like.

Compression: Before or After Recording... To Be or Not to Be

"Should I use a compressor while recording, or after I record?" This is a frequently asked, million-dollar question. First of all, it depends on the type of sound you are working on. For the sake of this example, let's consider a lead vocal as our subject sound.

I usually compress when recording ("going to tape") and I also compress the vocal on playback during the mix. This means I'm using the compressor as a preventative measure when first recording the vocal, to keep any loud notes from distorting when going to tape (into the DAW, then to hard drive).

When doing a final mix on the song, I again apply a compressor to the lead vocal, but I use the compressor extra aggressively to create a more cosmetic sound, putting a soft "mash" on the entire vocal that enables me to raise the overall level of the vocal nice and high in the mix without hurting the listener's ears.

COMPRESSING WHILE RECORDING

When first recording the vocal, I insert a compressor between the mic-pre and the recorder. My objective is not to compress the entire performance, but only to prevent any of the singer's really loud notes from distorting.

Think of a gymnast on a trampoline. Her routine will most likely include low hops, mid-level jumps, and really high leaps. If she gets especially inspired during her routine, she runs the risk of jumping so high that she could slam her head into the ceiling of the gym. This is not good. In order to allow her to get as spirited as she wants without injuring herself, we'll secure a mattress onto the ceiling of the gym to act as a cushion that will protect her from slamming her head on the ceiling.

We do not want the mattress hanging too low, because that will prevent her from doing her mid-height jumps. There is no danger of her hitting her head on the ceiling if she is jumping low or to her mid-level height. Only if she gets exceptionally spirited and jumps really high is she at risk of banging her head on the ceiling.

Obviously, the mattress represents a compressor, and the gymnast represents a vocal performance's fluctuating volume through the course of a song – loud, then soft, then midline, soft, then very loud, etc. If the ceiling (threshold) of the compressor is too low when recording the vocal, it will prevent the singer from delivering power to the song because the ceiling is allowing the the singer to jump only so high. If the ceiling is too low, the powerful notes will sound smashed and held down. This over-compressed sound on a recorded vocal is usually not a good sound and limits the flexibility of dialing in a really great sound later in the final mix.

In conclusion, when using a compressor while recording a vocal, it is wise to use it as a protective measure by keeping the really loud notes from hitting their head on the ceiling of the gym.

What does that look like in the real world?
Set your ratio knob to 3:1 or 4:1.

Make sure the VU needle is set to 0 (zero). If it is not, find a switch that makes the VU meter jump, from laying all the way to the left, over to zero. Turn the threshold knob all the way off, usually to the right, then ask the singer to hit some strong notes over and over so you can find a good ceiling height.

Next, begin lowering the threshold while the singer is repeatedly hitting the strong note. Once you see the VU needle start to jump (dance to the left a tad), you have found what I call the "point of intersection." Now ask the singer to alternate between hitting loud and soft notes. As you lower the ceiling a bit more, the needle should jump to the left when the strong notes are hit, *but any softly sung notes should not make the needle jump.* When you find this balance, you have a great compression setting for recording the vocal.

If the soft notes make the needle jump as far as the strong notes, then your threshold (ceiling) is *too low.* Raise it back up a bit. This would be the same as hanging a mattress so low from the gym ceiling that even if the gymnast hops twelve inches on the trampoline, she is bumping her head on the mattress.

COMPRESSING AFTER RECORDING

Once the vocal is delivered safe and clean to the recorder without distortion, it is frozen and stored on the hard drive in that pristine state. It has made it through the fire and has been delivered to the hard drive clean of distortion, thanks to the protective application of the compressor.

We used the compressor sparingly when we recorded – to deliver the most natural, unencumbered vocal performance possible. We have recorded a clean, robust vocal tone.

Let's say weeks have passed and now it is time to mix the song. When we mix, one of our main objectives, in addition to setting the levels, is to make sure each individual instrument and vocal performance sounds as good as it possibly can. We achieve this "dressing up" of each sound by using different devices such as:

• EQ
• Delay and/or reverb
• De-essing (softening any sound that has too much "sizzle")
• Chorus or flanging, etc.
• Compression

When we apply compression to the vocal during mixing, we use the compressor not as a protective device per se, like we did while recording it, but more as a cosmetic tool. In other words, it affects the vocal sounds, just as a woman who wears eyeliner creates a dramatic effect for her eyes.

Let's go further. When I apply compression to the vocal while mixing, I move the ceiling (threshold) lower than I would if I were recording the vocal, but I set the ratio to create a soft ceiling. Remember, the lower the ratio (2:1, 3:1, etc.), the softer the surface of the ceiling. (You might want to review fundamentals of compressors in an earlier section of this book.)

If I have a low ceiling in my racquetball court that is made of soft rubber, the ball will hit the ceiling more often and will be absorbed into the soft rubber, drastically affecting the game play. This is what I want when applying compression to my vocal while mixing. I want the vocal to push against the soft rubber barrier, creating a sort of cushion between the sound and the listener.

Think of sitting ringside at a boxing match. Thank goodness for the ropes that keep the fighters from falling into your lap and smashing you! If there were no elastic ropes, no one would be allowed to sit that close to the action.

The same goes when mixing the lead vocal. Without the elasticity of the compressor, we would not be able to get the vocal loud and up front in the mix. Without the elasticity, the vocal would need to be buried in the mix with the rest of the rhythm instruments, so that it would not jump out and nail the listener in the ear.

IN CONCLUSION

You can apply the same principles to any instrument. Generally speaking, going lighter on compression when recording is a good rule of thumb, because if you compress too much while recording, you are stuck with an over-compressed sound printed on the hard drive.

But if you know you want an overly compressed tone that gives the overall sound a certain desired effect, then have at it! For example, when recording room mics for drums, I'll purposely over-compress to create what many call the "John Bonham" sound.

At the end of the day, when recording, try and understand what it is you are going for in capturing a certain sound. Take a moment to think about how this sound is to fit into the overall collection of sounds in your production:

- What are you trying to achieve by recording this sound?
- Is it intended to be a rhythm element, or more of a lead line element?
- Do you want this sound to stand out, or to layer well with other sounds?

By asking yourself a few questions, you'll always know whether to compress for effect or for utility. There are no right or wrong answers when it comes to compression, but at the same time, you can do some real damage with one.

CHAPTER 10
MIKING TECHNIQUE

Microphone placement is not an exact science. There is no right or wrong way to place a mic on an instrument. The main rule of thumb is to take a moment to listen to the sound you want to record. Many people will just grab any ol' mic and set it up without really listening to the sound.

Take a moment and just listen. Ask yourself:

- Where is most of the sound coming from?

- Do I want the echo of the room, or just the close, dry sound of the instrument itself?
- Is it a loud sound coming from an amp or a quiet sound coming from an acoustic instrument?
- Do I need to use more than one mic in order to record multiple instruments simultaneously, as if miking up a drum set?

Generally speaking, if you're going to record something very loud, you should probably use a dynamic microphone. If you need to record multiple instruments that are close together – such as a snare, tom-tom, hi-hat, etc. – you should probably use dynamic mics so each mic picks up only the drum that is being miked and not the neighboring drums.

If you are recording something that is not amplified, you should probably use a condenser mic to pick up all details of the sound. This list includes:

- Vocals
- Violin

- Piano
- Acoustic guitar
- Guitar amp: six feet away from amp
- Bass amp: three feet away from amp
- Entire drum kit: in middle of room to capture the ambiance of the room, etc.

MIC PLACEMENT EXAMPLES

Guitar

Electric guitar (amp): Place a dynamic mic right up against the screen that covers the speaker. Remember, dynamic mics can handle very loud volumes. Also, you might place a condenser mic at least three feet or more away from the speaker to capture the ambiance of the room.

Acoustic guitar: Place a condenser mic near the sound hole, approximately nine to twelve away. Ask the guitarist to play as you place your ear close to the sound hole. Move your ear around the sound hole area to find the best-sounding spot.

Bass: Bass guitars can be recorded a few different ways:

First, it is wise to use a large-diaphragm dynamic mic on a bass speaker. Bass sound waves are much wider, so the bigger the pick-up area of the mic, the better the bass sound you will capture. My favorite large-diaphragm dynamic mic is the AKG-D112. It sounds great on bass amps and kick drums as well. Place the mic three inches or so away from the bass amp speaker.

AKG-D112

Also, try placing a condenser mic three to six feet away from the bass-amp speaker in order to capture the ambient room echo from the bass amp. When blending the close, dynamic mic sound with the condenser mic sound, you get a really great, full-bodied sonority.

Type 10 Direct Box

Using a Direct Box on the Bass

A Direct Box is an adaptor that allows you to connect a guitar cable (1/4 inch jack) to a microphone cable (XLR). Instead of plugging the bass guitar directly into the bass amp head, you plug the bass guitar into the Direct Box.

On the other side of the Direct Box there are usually two empty jacks. One is to connect to the bass amp head and the other jack is an XLR jack that you plug directly into a microphone pre-amp. The Direct Box allows you to split the bass signal into two, kind of like a "Y" cable. You send one to the amp and the other directly to a mic-pre.

Now you have a microphone on the bass amp speaker that picks up the sound of the amp and you also have the Direct Box plugged in to pick up the sound of the bass guitar itself. You will record the "mic" and the "Direct" signals on two separate tracks so that you have total control over each when you are ready to mix it all down.

Drums

Recording a drumset is an art form in and of itself. I love the challenge because every drumset is a unique collection and configuration of instruments. Take your time when miking a drum kit. If possible, allocate at least a few hours to do the job and get the sound right. Again, there is no right or wrong way to mic up drums, but here are some basic steps that should yield superior results:

- Choosing all the mics for each drum
- Placing mics on stands and wiring
- Placing each mic to each drum
- Plugging each mic into a mic-pre
- Getting mic sounds
- Adjusting microphone positioning on each drum to find the best sound

Selecting the right mic for each drum is a personal decision. Again, there is no right or wrong way, but I will suggest some mics that work well for me.

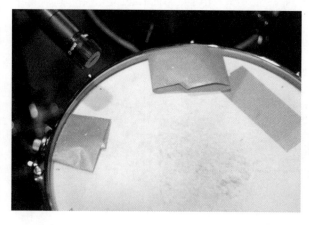

Snare drum: Shure SM-57 positioned about three to five inches above the snare head placed at a diagonal angle to the snare.

Do not put the mic too close to the snare. You will get a much richer, purer tone if you allow a bit of space between the mic and snare head. You can also aim a second dynamic mic at the bottom head of the snare to pick up more "rattle." Beware of "phasing," which is described just below.

Kick drum: A large diaphragm mic such as AKG-D112 just at the hole in the front of the kick. By front, I mean the side of the kick drum the audience sees. The D-112 (large-diaphragm dynamic mic) will give you the "thump" sound, which is the heart of your kick drum tone.

You can also add a large condenser mic one to three feet from the kick drum. This will give you an open, roomy sound when added to the thump of the D-112 in the hole.

Side Discussion – Phasing

Sometimes when you have two mics picking up the same sound, you may encounter them being "out of phase." The mics cancel each other out and – instead of creating a bigger sound together – create a nasty, thin sound.

This can be fixed either by hitting the "phase switch" on the mic-pre or EQ (which has a zero with a diagonal line through it), or simply by moving one of the mics a short distance away from the other.

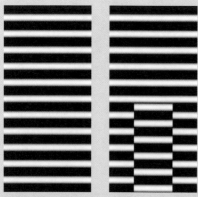

Left is In Phase, right is Out of Phase.

Phase button (inset)

Okay, back to miking…

Hi-Hat: Use any pencil or regular-diaphragm dynamic or condenser mic for the hi-hat. Aim it about four to five inches above the top of the hi-hat. Be sure to position the mic to the hi-hat with the hi-hat in the open position. If you place the mic with the pedal depressed, the hi-hat may hit the mic when the drummer opens the hi-hat during recording.

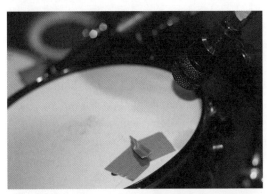

Toms: A great mic for toms is the Sennheiser 421. These work very well on toms because they have a bigger diaphragm than a standard dynamic mic and pick up better "lows." Toms have lots of low end. Pan the small tom to the left, the middle tom to the center, and the floor tom to the right, to create a spatial stereo effect.

Cymbals: Using condenser mics overhead always works well. Place one mic about six feet above the hi-hat and the other about six feet above the floor tom. Aim both mics so they are pointing at the drummer's head.

These two mics are sent to two separate tracks in your recorder. On your mixer, pan the condenser mic above the hi-hat all the way to the left and the other mic over the floor tom all the way to the right. This will give you a cool stereo effect – a really nice, spatial sound.

Room mics: You can have fun with room mic choice and placement. Any condenser or tube mic will work. If you have some mics left over, try experimenting with different combinations of room mics. You can use one, two, three, or even four mics placed in different parts of the room to capture many cool, unique combinations of sounds. The sky is the limit.

John Bonham's drum sound from Led Zeppelin epitomizes a first-rate "room sound." Guitarist Jimmy Page produced Led Zeppelin and at times recorded the drums in a castle. Castles usually have thick stone walls that reflect sound and add a certain warm tone. So, the surfaces of the walls in your recording room play a big part in the overall sonority you get.

If you are working in a room with surfaces that reflect lots of sound (hard surfaces like concrete, wood, stone, etc.), be creative. Tape blankets to the walls if you have to! The thicker the material you have, the more sound that will be absorbed. On the other hand, if your room is real dead-sounding because you have carpet on the walls, you can liven up the room by leaning sheets of wood against the walls. Again, be creative! There is no right way or wrong way to get a unique sound. Do whatever it takes to capture a compelling and unique tone.

RECORDING VOCALS

When recording vocals, put your vocalist in as small and as tight-sounding a room as possible. If you have to, tape blankets to the walls of a closet or bathroom to create a tight sound. Nowhere is it written that a bathroom cannot be an effective vocal booth. A decent, large-diaphragm condenser mic will sound great for vocals, regardless of the vocal style.

It is important to use a "popper-stopper" between the mic and the vocalist. The "four-fingers" measuring method is a reliable way to figure how much distance there should be between the mic and the popper-stopper. You should be able to put four fingers (imagine a karate chop) between the mic and the popper-stopper.

Re-amping

Re-amping is a way to turn a mundane sound into something really cool. Let's say you have a keyboard sound recorded from one of the virtual synths in your DAW. It sounds okay, but you are not jumping up and down with joy over it.

Re-amping is running that bland keyboard sound out of the computer using a guitar cable into another room and plugging the other end into an actual guitar amp.

Once this sound is playing out of the guitar amp, you put a mic (or combination of mics) on the amp and then record it on another track back into your DAW.

This is so much fun because the room containing the amp creates the ambiance and is picked up by the mics. Now that bland keyboard sound has a live feel. Try it on everything. It works very well.

VIRTUAL GUITARS AND AMPS

If you do end up recording some cool parts with a guitar modeler, understand that the distortion sound is not being recorded. Only the raw, plinky guitar sound that is coming directly out of your guitar is being laid down. The effected sound from the amp modeler is only being temporarily laid on top of your raw guitar sound. Think of it as a mask. You can put it on and take it off anytime, but your original, ugly face is always there under the mask.

The advantage is this: You are not stuck with that one distortion sound you first used. Later, if you want to hear some other effect on that specific recorded guitar part, you can bypass or remove the amp you have had on there and replace it with a new one. A possible scenario: When you first recorded the guitar, you thought the song might go in one creative direction, but as the song evolves, you realize that the first distortion sound you started with is not right for this new direction.

Additionally, you have the option of permanently "burning" any guitar track down to a new track using an amp modeler. This is called "printing," which is when you internally record one track to another. This way, you never run the risk of losing a particular effected sound.

"How might I lose the perfect sound?" you ask. Many times, different folks have different versions of the same DAW software. Occasionally, some of the effects in an older version will not be recognized by a newer one, and vice versa.

If you know that you will be working on a song in someone else's studio, and you started on your older (or newer) software at home, you might want to bounce those tracks with really special effects on them to new tracks so that the effects and their original sounds are all married together. Don't worry; you can always go back to your own system and have access to the original, unbounced tracks. And that is a blessing.

CHAPTER 11
MIXING

Like miking, mixing is an art form unto itself. To understand the basic fundamentals of mixing means to create better mixes from the very outset. Mixing in a DAW basically mirrors the same principles of mixing on a real console (mixing board). So first, let's break down an audio mixing console into simple parts:

- Channels
- Stereo-bus

Just like all cars have the same basic equipment (steering wheel, engine, ignition/key, doors, gas pedal, brake, etc.), mixing boards always have at least **channels** and a **stereo-bus section**.

Each individual sound/instrument runs through its own channel, then all channels are funneled into the stereo-bus section, which leads to the outside world (CD burner, hard drive, speakers).

Here's a simple illustration: Imagine a bunch of cars trying to leave the parking lot of a sports arena after a football game. Chaos. Vehicles approaching from every angle must file into a two-lane path to go out the gate and head home. There is a person at the merge waving a flag, signaling drivers to either hurry up or slow down as they file in line and approach the passage out. The flagger does this to maximize the movement of the autos, keeping them moving at a steady rate.

In this analogy, the cars represent sounds moving through the channels of a mixing board, and the two-lane path to exit represents the stereo-bus.

- Stereo: For our purposes, stereo means two paths, left and right.
- Bus: Think of a city transit bus that carries people from one place to another.
- Stereo-bus: Two lanes leading out of the console.

Every stereo bus section has a "stereo bus meter." These are the two VU (or LED) meters that dance back and forth or up and down; they are usually positioned at the center of the mixing board.

Think of the stereo bus meter as the speedometer of the mixing board. Just as a car speedometer shows how fast you are going, the stereo bus meter tells you how much signal is pumping out of the console to the outside world (CD burner, tape machine, hard drive, etc.).

THE FIRST STEP

On an analog console, the stereo bus meters are usually right in the middle of the console on the bridge, the area that slopes up a bit on the console. But in order to have a stereo bus section in a DAW, one

Stereo bus meter

sometimes must create it. This is done in Pro Tools by clicking on the "track" icon in menu at top, and selecting "stereo" > "master fader." Now, all the channels in your session funnel through this stereo-bus channel. This main channel's fader should be set to zero (0), which is called "unity gain." (Zero/unity is about 3/4 the way up; take a look.)

Notice that this stereo-bus channel may have two sets of numbers:

1. A vertical row next to fader ranging from "infinity to 12" (in Pro Tools)
2. A second vertical row next to vertical LED meter ranging from -60 to 0" (in Pro Tools)

Now your session is set up like an analog console, and you are ready to begin mixing.

THE NEXT STEP

So let's say you are ready to begin mixing a song. You have a full session loaded in. The session contains, for instance:

- 12 tracks of drums (kick drum, snare top and bottom mics, three toms, hi-hat, two overhead mic tracks, three room-mic tracks)
- Three bass guitar tracks (one dynamic mic on bass amp speaker, one condenser mic five feet away from bass amp, one Direct Box channel)
- Six tracks of stereo rhythm and solo guitars
- Eight tracks of keyboards of all types
- 12 tracks of vocals, including lead and background vocals
- Three stereo tracks of sound effects and special production elements

All the channel faders are pulled all the way down, and the stereo-bus fader is set to unity-zero. You are now ready to push the first sound up and begin. Which fader should you push up first?

The kick drum fader is a great place to start. Think of the kick drum as the foundation of the mix, just as a slab of concrete is the foundation for a house. Push the kick drum fader up. But how far?

Mix principle: Push the kick drum fader up until it makes the stereo-bus LED meter rise three-quarters of the way up to "-3" (just below -6). This may not make sense right now, but as we move forward, it will.

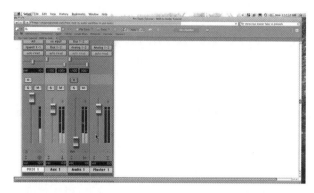

Stereo bus fader

Before setting the level of any sound, you first should make sure it is as polished as it can be. More on this in a bit.

When the mix is finished, you want your stereo bus LED meter to be hitting at approximately "-3." This is the reason we pushed the first sound (kick drum) up so it made the stereo-bus meter hit around "-6." This way, we left enough extra space on the speedometer (stereo-bus) for all the remaining sounds/tracks to be added without them pushing the stereo bus into the red.

We always want to leave some extra room (head room) on the stereo-bus (about three dB) so that when we hand the mix off to a mastering engineer, he or she has a little room (between -3 and 0 at the top) to tweak the mix further. (See the chapter on mastering for more information.)

Important note: As stated earlier, for each sound you pull up, before setting the level, you should first make sure it sounds as compelling as it can be. Often, your first step in achieving this is by using an EQ to shape the sound. (Please review our discussion of the Magic Frequencies in the engineering chapter.)

To review:

- 100–120 Hz   clean low-end
    - add 2dB

- 200 Hz   muddy
    - "beer belly"
    - reduce by 2dB

- 2kHz   presence
    - sounds "pointy"
    - add 2dB to add attack, e.g., snare or kick drum
    - reduce 2dB to reduce nasally megaphone tone;
        e.g., heavy metal guitars or annoying voices

- 6kHz   definition
    - brings out "eyes"
    - add 1dB for tone clarity

- 10kHz   sizzle
    - "lip gloss"
    - add a little shine
    - add 2dB for a touch of brightness

You can achieve setting these frequencies using any five-band parametric equalizer. These Magic Frequencies work so well that you can use them on any type of sound:

- Vocal
- Snare drum
- Kick drum
- Guitar, acoustic or electric
- Piano
- Synthesizer, etc.

SOME HELPFUL HINTS

If you're new to EQing, try applying these frequencies to a given sound, then click the "bypass" switch on the EQ on and off to hear the difference between the dry and EQ'd tone. From here, adjust according to what you feel is either lacking or what is overdone. Use your instincts; take a moment and really listen without distraction. You will get a gut feeling one way or another if you really concentrate.

After shaping the sound with EQ, you may choose to use one or a combination of many different plug-in tools to further enhance the given sound.

- *Compressor:* To add more snap to the sound of a snare or kick drum; to soften the overall edginess of a guitar tone; add to a lead vocal to create a soft, protective barrier between the lead vocal and the listener to get the lead vocal nice and loud in the mix without hurting the listener's ear. (Refer to the section on compressors in the engineering chapter.)
- *De-Esser:* Used to compress sizzly frequencies such as the shrill of a cymbal crash; lessens bright "sss" sounds on a lead vocal.
- *Harmonic plug-ins:* Add a distortion plug-in to a sound to give it "sharp teeth"; give another sound a lo-fi tone, etc.
- *Modulation plug-ins:* You may choose to apply a vibrating effect such as a flanger or a chorus to a given sound to make it sound wider; to add depth to a given sound, etc. You can use these devices to simply make it sound weirder or more unique, too.
- *Time-based plug-ins:* These are effects such as reverb and delay that create depth and space. There are both "colored" and "transparent" reverbs and

delays. Colored means the effect has a unique tone in and of itself such as an old, analog device may sound, as opposed to a transparent one that simply copies the sound and plays it later in time, adding no unusual color; it's an exact mirror image. Actually, just about all devices can be categorized as either colored or transparent.

- *Sound-field effects:* These usually have to do with spatial, left-to-right imaging; places an element in a particular spot in the left-right/front-back, 3D space that is your mix environment. Some imagers allow you to place a sound wider than where the actual speakers are physically sitting. This is usually achieved applying principles of "psycho-acoustics."
- *Pitch-shift plug-ins:* Running sounds through a "pitch-and-tune" device in real time, while the actual session is running, can create many unique effects. The sky is the limit.

Personally, I usually do all my pitch and tuning work separately during editing (prep and tweak time before I begin mixing), instead of allowing the tune device to run by itself while printing the mix. Doing it during editing gives me more control of the outcome of the tuning instead of random defaulting of the tune device while running in real time.

In conclusion, regarding effects: First dress up each sound as you see fit, using any of the devices above, *then* set the level of the given sound. Let's say the first sound we want to deal with is the kick drum. For starters, we want to get the kick drum sounding great on its own. Once we like the gadgets we have placed on it, we adjust the kick drum fader so it makes the stereo-bus LED meter rise to just below "-6."

If the kick drum was recorded using two or more microphones (maybe one in the hole, and one on the beater side), then:

1. Get each kick track sounding the best it can on its own.
2. Blend these separate tracks together, bringing each fader up against the others.
3. Once you have a great blend of these separate tracks, "group" them together so that when you move one of the faders, the other kick mic faders follow accordingly and you maintain this unique blend of kick drum tracks.
4. Set this grouped cluster of kick drum mics so they make the stereo-bus LED meter rise up to just below "-6."

After the kick drum level is set so the stereo-bus LED rises to "-6," bring up the snare drum.

First, *solo* the snare so you can hear it alone without the kick drum. Dress up the snare using plug-ins as you see fit, then un-solo the snare and (using only your ears) adjust the snare fader so it plays back evenly with the kick drum. This is where your ears take over; it is up to you to decide how high or low to place the level of the snare with the kick drum.

I like to start out using these two specific elements (kick and snare) because they act as counter balances of each other. Once you have established a favorable balance between these two, the remaining tracks you bring up one by one will fall right into place easier than if you did not have a solid kick-snare balance.

Here is the usual order in which I bring up each sound in a given mix:
1. Kick drum(s)
2. Snare(s) (sometimes a top and bottom mic)
3. Hi-hat
4. Toms
   a. Tom 1 (high rack), pan left
   b. Tom 2 (mid rack), leave in center
   c. Tom 3 (floor tom), pan right
5. Drum overhead mics (pan left and right)
6. Drum room mics (pan left and right according to where mics were placed in room)
7. Any remaining random drum mics
8. Bass guitar or bass keyboard
   a. Direct-Box track (DI)
   b. Any mics on bass amp
9. Main musical instrument in given song, such as
   a. Piano
   b. Guitar
   c. Synth sound
10. Pad elements
   a. Guitar rhythm layers (pan left and right accordingly)
   b. Keyboard supporting layers (pan left and right accordingly)
11. Lead vocals
12. Background vocals (pan left and right accordingly)
13. Any solo instruments (guitar or key solos, etc.)
14. Any sound effects elements and candy (pan left or right accordingly)

Step-by-Step Mix Principles Overview
1. Pull up kick drum(s); dress it up using EQ, compression, and or other plug-ins; next, place kick drum faders so they make stereo bus LED meter rise up to just below "-6" (or 3/4 the way up to "-3"). *Do not* touch the kick drum any more from this point on for the rest of the mix; bring all remaining sounds up to the kick.
2. Solo snare drum track(s); dress it/them up using EQ, compression, and or any of the plug-ins listed above; then use your ears to place it at a nice level against the kick drum. *Do not* touch the kick drum level; only adjust snare level *to* the kick drum.

3. Solo the hi-hat; dress it up according to taste; use your ears to place it at a level appropriate to kick and snare level.
4. Solo up tom 1 track; dress it up to taste; place it against already established sounds.
5. Continue same routine for all remaining sounds, one by one.

There is an infinite number of combinations of plug-ins you can apply to each of these elements listed above, too many to go into here.

GHETTO STEREO

A cool technique for widening any sound is to adopt a simple technique I call "ghetto stereo." Let's say you have a piano that was recorded using only one microphone. Boring. Pianos are full of texture and width, so using only one mic is indeed limiting the potential of the overall sound – unless you are going for a "lo-fi" vibe.

If you are mixing a song and discover that the piano is on only one track, try this:
1. Make a duplicate of the piano track.
2. Pan the original piano track all the way to the left, and the duplicate to the right.
3. Insert a delay plug-in on the duplicate track only.
4. Set the delay settings to:
    a. mix: 100 percent
    b. delay time: 35 ms (milliseconds)
    c. feedback: 0
5. Group the original and duplicate piano tracks together.

Now you have created a pseudo-stereo effect for the single piano track, thus giving the piano a much wider sound and feel. This works on *any* single instrument, even vocals.

AUTOMATION

After you have gone through the entire process of first dressing up a sound, setting its level to the rest of the mix, it is time to automate some of the channels. *Automation* is simply telling the computer to move the sound on a given channel either up or down, on or off, left or right, or any combination at specific points during the song. Often, the mixer needs to "ride" the vocal volume up at certain spots (and down at others) in order to create a uniform lead vocal level as it plays over different parts of a song.

This "riding" of a fader also applies to turning the channel either on or off (muting) at spots, and also riding the "panner" switch either left, right, or somewhere in between. Programming each channel with combinations of automated instructions

Side note: In the top bar of ProTools, click the "window" icon, then scroll down to "automation." Click it and a window pops up. Make sure all the little boxes are clicked red. This activates the entire system for automation.

is what really gives a mix maximum production value; this really adds lots of exciting bells and whistles to a mix.

Automation in Pro Tools is very simple: You switch the automation window on a given channel from "read" to "trim." (There are other automation modes available, but I prefer using "trim.") When "trim" is engaged, the fader, panner, and mute button are all "live." Using the mouse, touch one of these buttons (fader, mute, pan switch) and you are "writing" automation. Simply let go and the channel remembers the moves you just made. When you play that same section of song back where you touched a switch while in "trim," you will see that button move on its own.

There are certain sounds that usually require automation more than others. Some of these are:
- Lead vocals
- Guitar solos
- Synth lead lines
- Cymbal crashes
- DJ scratch elements
- Certain percussion elements
- Drum fills
- Vocal ad-lib tracks

Some sounds overall may be louder in a mix, while others are tucked behind as support elements. Think of a band onstage. When a member moves to the front of the stage at a given moment, his sound increases while the other members recede into the background – until another featured sound takes its place. Imagining this gives the rookie mixer a perspective as to how the mix may ebb and flow from start to finish.

It is purely up to the taste of the mixer, which is why mixing is such an incredible art form. I strongly suggest using references; try to get your mix sounding sonically similar to one you love. A/B back and forth between your mix and the reference periodically to see how yours is shaping up.

WHAT TO PRINT WHEN READY TO MIX

Now you are ready to "print" the mix. To print means to record the mix to a stereo (left/right) file. WAV and AIFF files are standard, full-fidelity file types. WAV (Microsoft) and AIFF (Apple) files are basically interchangeable. They are both CD quality, as opposed to mp3 files, which are "data compressed" and don't sound as good. But since mp3s are smaller than WAV and AIFF files, they are easily sent via email.

Most folks nowadays simply print the mix down to a hard drive, but some prefer to record the mix down to an analog device such as a 1/2-inch or 1/4-inch tape machine. Obviously, printing to actual tape is costly, approximately 65 dollars per reel, and you get only about 16 minutes; that comes out to be about four to five prints per reel. Even though tape can be expensive, many love the sound that actual magnetic tape provides, as opposed to bouncing it down internally to a hard drive.

ANALOG VERSUS DIGITAL

There is an ongoing debate between analog and digital. Think of analog this way: You are speeding down the freeway and bugs splat against your front windshield. Some bugs nick the windshield and may leave a little stain, others hit dead-on and you see their last expression on their little insect face permanently staring at you, while still others were coming in way too fast and leave a huge splotch across your windshield.

These three different degrees of splotch (nicked, straight hit, annihilate) can visually represent how an electron/magnetic-charge (sound) physically smashes into analog tape. Analog, magnetic tape is an "art" medium, meaning "hitting" the tape at different degrees of hardness actually changes the sound.

Not sending enough signal to tape can equate to a diminished tone. Hitting the tape square on is how the tape should be hit, thus giving you optimum performance of the tape. But we artists/engineers never adhere to the word "should." Thus, we have the option also of hitting the tape super hard, which achieves saturation or "tape compression." It's like over-exposing film to too much light; it creates a hazy, saturated look. For a beginner, this can be a nightmare, but for the consummate professional, this is living the dream.

Now imagine the same bugs flying into the windshield, but with a little guy on the hood of the car snapping a sequence of pictures of the bug and colliding with the windshield. This is digital.

Later, when you stop the car and wash the bugs off, the bugs on the windshield are bumpy and textured, as opposed to the photos, which look exactly like the real thing. But there is no "texture" like the dried up bugs on the windshield, only the smooth surface of the pictures. This is just a thought exercise to wrap your head around the concept, not a literal translation.

You can also think of the difference between analog and digital like this:
- *Analog:* Actual materials touching each other; for example: turntable needle on vinyl or audio tape rubbing against tape machine playback heads. Noise is a by-product of this rubbing and touching
- *Digital:* No actual touching materials per se; for example: a laser lighting pits on a CD. There is digital audio tape, but heads are reading digital info encoded on the tape, then translating it. It is not "analogous" to the actual sound, but a facsimile of it.

A needle dragging against the groove of a record creates a scraping sound similar to that of a hanging car muffler dragging against the street. It's not a pretty sound, but when scaled up, the "white noise" created by contact between turntable needle and record is laced under the playback music.

One would think this would be bad, having noise under the music, but we humans live in an ambient world. Rarely are we in a totally soundproof space, and when we are, it feels and sounds very strange. You can think of the white noise under the music as a connector of the individual sounds in the music, gluing everything together. Melted cheese between two hamburger patties comes to mind; not the healthiest, but oh so tasty!

In essence, then, you can think of white noise as melted cheese for your music. Are we saying that digital must be like wheat germ – dry and tasteless? No, digital has its advantages as well, such as exact playback every time with no loss of fidelity; replication advantages; transmission between locations; significant reduction of cost to store mountains of data, etc.

It is a tradeoff, as are most things in life. There are advantages and disadvantages to both analog and digital.

Various mixes to print:

- Main mix: The full mix as you completed it.
- Lead vocal up mix: Raise lead vocal up a few dB, then print full mix again. Often, when you get to the mastering lab, you may discover the "vocal up" version is better.
- TV mix: The main mix, but with the *lead vocal muted*. This is used many times by artists when performing live to the track (no band). Leave all the backing vocals and ad libs on.
- Instrumental: Mute all the vocals, leads, backing, and ad libs. Music-only print.
- A cappella: Just opposite of instrumental. Print all vocals only, and remember not to mute any channels that are transmitting vocal effects like delay, reverb, etc.

When in mastering, the engineer may ask if you have both instrumental and *a cappella* prints of a given song. He can import both these versions side by side and now have separate control over the instrumentals and the vocals. He can fix any instrumental to vocal discrepancies you may have missed during mixing.

CHAPTER 12
MASTERING

There are two types of mastering, in my opinion:
- Full-Blown Mastering-Lab Mastering
- In-the-Box Ghetto Mastering

FULL-BLOWN MASTERING-LAB MASTERING

Let's say you are a producer and you have a body of work consisting of ten songs. All ten mixes sound amazing individually. As a producer, you wouldn't have approved them if they didn't. But when you listen to them one after another, they sound like ten totally random, separate pieces, not a unified body of work. Why? Primarily because the "Sonic (EQ) and Volume Uniformity" is not there, among other factors.

Having a body of work consisting of perhaps three, five, or ten songs, most likely you will want to take this body of work to a mastering engineer. This engineer will listen to your songs and focus on four main concepts:
- EQing
- Levels
- Sequencing
- Spacing between songs

EQing

The mastering engineer will first take these different mixes and dump them into mastering software (a specialized DAW for mastering). The mastering program WaveLab is very popular. Standing alone, all these mixes sound superb, but when played back-to-back, they're completely disjunct. This is because some songs may have more electric guitar, which may give the total mix a sizzly presence, as opposed to other songs being beat-driven; this creates an overall low-end tone to the mix.

The main objective of the mastering engineer is to get all these songs to sound uniform. He may do this by listening to 35–40 seconds of each song and finding one that sounds well-balanced enough to use as a template for the rest. The highs, mids, and lows of this particular song sound well-rounded and generally have a good perspective. (You know, the Goldilocks rule of "not too hot, not too cold… just right.") He may shape the highs, mids, and/or lows of this template mix a bit more to embellish the compelling attributes of this template mix a bit farther.

The process begins by playing one of the remaining nine songs against this model song. Doing this, he will know whether to add or take away bass, mid-range, or high-end frequencies to make this new selection sound sonically similar to the model. Then he continues on from there with the remaining songs.

It is important that you EQ before setting levels (discussed in next step). EQing adds and/or takes away treble, mid-range, and/or bass. If you establish a level for a song, then start adding or taking away bass, treble, or mid-range, this will increase or decrease the level you just set. You will have to backtrack and reset your level.

Setting Levels

The objective of setting levels is to enable the listener to enjoy the songs back to back at an even, continuous volume. The quietest part of the quietest song should be as audible as the loudest part of the loudest song. The listener should never have to lean into the speakers to hear the quieter moments nor move away from the speakers during the louder. This does not mean that everything is going to be exactly the same volume. It is much subtler than that.

Two devices that help establish level are compressors and limiters. I like to think of a compressor as a forgiving limiter. Think of the ropes of a boxing ring. They are flexible. If a boxer falls into the ropes, they bend with his weight. This is a compressor. When using a limiter, however, the ropes would be wooden. They do not flex nearly as much. There would be no bend in the ropes for the boxer with a limiter. A compressor is going to "give" elastically while a limiter will not.

When speaking of levels, let's take a moment to talk about the concepts of "dynamic range" and "headroom" and how they apply. We understand these concepts theoretically, but let's demystify them.

"Dynamic range" basically means differences in volume; it is the difference between the highest and lowest volumes in a piece of music. Let's say you are listening to orchestral music. You hear the loud banging of the timpani, which then moves into a soft flute melody, followed by a full orchestral sonority and then back again to a quiet moment. This is an example of wide dynamic range.

In order to push the level (volume) of a song up so it plays back nice and loud from a CD, it is probably a good idea to use either a compressor or a limiter to avoid distorting the level in case you raise the volume too much. But the more the level is raised, the more the possibility you will reach a point where you start to lose dynamic range.

What does this mean – to begin to lose dynamic range the more you raise the level? Well, think of it this way: You're in a room and suddenly it begins to fill with water. A point occurs where the water gets so high that in order for you to keep your head above water and breathing, you begin to tread water.

From this unfortunate point, you rise as the water rises. The water level represents the level of the song we are raising. As the room quickly fills, you rise closer and closer to the ceiling of the room. This breathing space between the water level and the ceiling can be appropriately called the "headroom."

This headroom air space between the rising water level and the room's ceiling determines how much dynamic range you have available. (Remember, dynamic range basically means the range of volume between the softest and loudest moments in a given song.)

Think of the ceiling as the point of distortion. In order to prevent distorting, we place a barrier just before this distortion point so the song will not cross this line. This barrier is a "limiter." Without this barrier, the hairdo of the song may poke past this point and we will hear distortion.

Back to headroom…

Determine what kind of music you are trying to optimize:

- Music with wide dynamic-range? e.g., classical, jazz, etc. (big differences in volume from section to section)
- A more modern music style with narrow dynamic range? e.g., heavy metal, hip-hop, electronica, etc. (music with only one volume: loud!)

If you are mastering a jazz piece with alternating quiet and loud moments and you raise the "water level" so high that you leave no air space between the water and the ceiling, you lose all of your quiet moments. At this point, the quiet moments are now as loud as the loud moments. Yes, it will play louder from the CD, but you have sacrificed the quiet moments in the song, which conveys an abundance of emotion and pacing.

Conversely, if you are working with music with narrow dynamic range, you have the luxury of raising the level so high that the air space between the water level and the room's ceiling meet. This is because you don't have to worry about any quiet moments; the entire song is one volume: loud. Think of a pancake; it's flat. Only a pancake can fit in the narrow space between the high water level and the room's ceiling.

Sequencing

It is usually the producer, artist, and/or record label rep's job to determine the final order the songs are to play in, not the mastering engineer. Let's explore sequencing.

A cool way to help you figure out the best order of songs for your album is to create a few different song orders and burn each to a separate CD. Carry these CDs with you everywhere. Live with them. Let them marinate in your brain. Play them at home, play them constantly while driving in your car, listen to them periodically over a given number of days or weeks. After a bit, you will intuitively begin to feel what order is best. Doing the above will pay off.

Put your best songs first. Obviously, "best" is subjective, but here it refers to the song that epitomizes, the song that exemplifies what the group is all about. During the writing and recording process, there is often one song that naturally stands out from the rest, one song that random visitors to your studio and onlookers always seem to comment on. (Onlookers? These are guests who happen to visit during the weeks or months you are in the recording process.) Sometimes this standout song may not be your personal favorite, but as producer you must be objective enough to weigh all factors.

Be open to this information. Be conscious of who is making what comments. Is it young people, or an older consensus? Mostly male or female? We are always susceptible to losing objectivity to the music we are working on since we work so close to it. By keeping an open ear, these random comments by onlookers will help keep you objective.

Again, a heavily commented-on song might not be your personal favorite, but you must be objective and say to yourself, "I have to put the one first that is going to grab the listener." You must know what your market is, who your listeners are. Young girls? Cool dudes? Nerdy dudes? Single mothers? Angry men? Who?

Many times, though, it is the second and third songs on the album that crystallize, in the listener's head, who the artist really is. If you don't want the audience to pigeonhole your artist immediately into a category, create a song order that walks your listener down a specific path. Think of it as if you were walking through a garden with someone who is blind. Would you choose to walk them through pungent-scented vines first or through the lovely smelling gardenias at the start of your walk? The order is crucial in unfolding who the artist truly is to a new listener.

Spacing Between Songs

There is a huge difference between one-fourth of a second and three-fourths of a second if you are listening for it. When playing a CD, you come to the end of a song and anticipate the next song to begin, but if the empty space between is too long, you are thrown off for a moment. The mastering engineer left too much space between these particular songs and therefore dissipated the connective energy between them.

Ever hear dead air on the radio – you know, when there is a two-second gap of silence? It rarely happens, especially on commercial radio, but when it does, it seems odd.

Conventional wisdom suggests that the less silence you have between songs, the more captivated you'll keep the listener. This primarily appeals to more contemporary styles of music. Classical music may utilize more space between selections to allow the listener to fully absorb what they just heard before continuing to the next piece of music.

There is no right or wrong when applying space between songs. Generally speaking, though, try to keep your spacing short, and use more space to create dramatic effect between, for example, a heavy rocking song and a ballad.

IN-THE-BOX GHETTO MASTERING

To be honest, this is a name I made up to describe a certain shortcut approach to mastering. It means to push the level up and add as much EQ as possible so that a given mix can stand on its own and really sizzle.

This approach has evolved from the steady development of more and more sophisticated DAW plug-ins such as easy-to-use mastering limiters and EQs. Plug-in developers Waves, FabFilter, and iZotope are pioneers of such virtual devices, where one simply pulls down one switch ("threshold" knob) and hears the overall level of the mix increase without clipping (distortion). One-step mastering. But these devices in the wrong hands is like putting a bazooka in the hands of maniac – it's very easy to do damage.

How do we determine whether to do full-blown mastering-lab or in-the-box ghetto mastering? There is no hard rule on anything in this regard, only principles, and if you understand various principles, then you can make proper choices to suit your specific needs. If you know only one way to do a certain thing, then obviously your choices of approach are limited, so I offer different ways to present your music.

As stated in an earlier section, mastering was traditionally a specialized process performed by skilled engineers using optimized gear. Its goal was to create uniformity between the songs, not simply to push the volume of each mix as high as possible. But with the constant evolution of DAW plug-ins, folks have figured out ways to quickly maximize overall level and sonic performance without going to a full-blown mastering lab.

After completing the recording of a series of songs, a producer will mix one song at a time. Once a song is mixed, it is set aside and the next one is mixed, and so on. The time between mixing songs can vary from as little as a day or as long as a year. In every case, though, a producer obviously will not approve a given mix as finished unless he feels it sounds first-rate.

So then, after all the songs are mixed, they are taken to the mastering lab to all be lined up sonically, volume-wise, and so forth. But let's say you want to play the mixes for someone before they are mastered, which might not be taking place for weeks or months? You let the listener know that this song is mixed but not yet mastered; it is still possibly missing a little extra sizzle or tightening up.

But ironically, sometimes after mastering, a mix may seem as if it has been diminished. This is a common syndrome with newer producers. The original mix may have a huge, booming low-end and lots of overall level, but both may need to be scaled back just a tad (or even a good amount) in mastering in order for the song to sound compatible with the rest of the songs in the body of work.

In the 1990s, mastering-lab mastering took a quantum leap in its ability to raise the overall level of a mix, due to innovations in high-end mastering gear. A virtual arms race began as each mastering engineer strove to get his latest project to play louder than the last loud record that recently hit the streets.

This mentality of loud mixes became all pervasive as DAWs began to creep into the music industry in the late 1990s. Immediately, DAWs became a mainstay in the early 2000s as studio owners sold their two-inch analog tape machines for a fraction of what they paid for them to buy Pro Tools and other popular DAWs.

It was not long after that folks began to "doctor up" their mixes in Pro Tools by importing their analog mixes (still printed to 1/4" and 1/2" analog tape in early 2000s) into a "new session" in Pro Tools, adding a limiter and EQ to the stereo-master fader, pushing the level up and adding some high sizzle and some low-end, then "bouncing" this hot-rodded mix down internally so they could play these cool mixes for folks before they went to final mastering in the future.

It was a quick way of letting someone hear your pristine mixes all dressed up and pumped full of steroids. The ironic thing is: it stuck! People began to use these ghetto, mock-up masters as the final mastered mix.

The next problem was that now producers were taking these souped-up mixes into the real mastering lab to assemble the entire record, but the mastering engineers could not add their magic to the mixes because all the room in the level of the mix had been maxed out already. Since the level had been pushed up and additional EQ was added, there was already too much makeup on the model for the real mastering engineer to add any love. Really, the only thing he could do was reduce the level and reduce some of the EQ. In essence, he had to first work backward in order to move forward.

What is one to do then? Here's what I suggest:

1. Print your mixes with no (or very little) limiting or EQ on the master fader. I call these "pristine mixes."
2. Print a second pass of the mix with as much limiting and EQ as you want.
3. Play the hot-rodded prints for whomever you want, but when it's time to master the record for real, deliver the pristine prints to the mastering lab.

How to Ghetto-Master a Mix

There is no exact science to it. You can approach it in a couple of ways, either one song – or more than one song – at a time.

MASTERING ONE SONG

Do your mix, and before you bounce to disc, open up a stereo-master fader (if you have not done so already) and insert the best EQ plug-in and limiter you have onto the master channel. The order in which the plug-ins are inserted does make a difference.

1. EQ first, then limiter: This way, the EQ will be getting squashed by the limiter, so you can be much more aggressive with the EQ. I usually rock it in this order because I like the EQ to agitate the limiter and get more of a pumping sound and feel; it comes off a little more aggressive.

2. Limiter first, then EQ: The pristine mix is limited in order to raise the overall level, then the EQ makes up the difference of what got smashed by the limiter. Think of putting small tacks (EQ) with the pointy ends pointing out onto a smooth surface ("limited" mix). You have to be more conservative with the EQ since there is nothing to limit (hold back) these pointy frequencies you are adding and it may cause the mix to start clipping.

Experiment with both. There is no right or wrong, only this to remember: If it sounds good to you, then it is good for you. Hopefully, you have solid instincts, so that what you hear is what the public likes also. There are many geniuses who are commercially unsuccessful, simply because their genius does not appeal to the masses, but to only a small, distinguished group.

MASTERING MORE THAN ONE SONG

If you have a few mixes done and want to put a ghetto mastering process on all of them so you can play them back to back, follow this recipe:

1. Open a "new session" in your DAW, then "import" the mixes (preferably WAV or AIFF files) into the session.
2. Create a "stereo-master fader." Place all faders including master fader to "unity" gain, which is 0 (zero).
3. Solo one song and listen to it. Insert an EQ onto that channel. Try adding my Magic Frequencies:
   - add 2dB of 120Hz
   - take away 1 dB of 200Hz
   - add 1/2dB of 2kHz
   - add 1dB of 6kHz
   - add 2dB of 10kHz
   - filter off 2dB from 0Hz up to 50Hz
4. Notice how much room you have left on the stereo fader meter. If you have some space between the top of the LED and the red at very top, then you can begin to slowly lower the "threshold" knob on the limiter. If you are using a limiter designed for DAW mastering, like the Waves L2 Limiter, this will be easy for you.
5. Step back and listen for a moment before doing anything else. See if you hear any distortion or if anything is out of proportion. It should sound like the mix just got pumped with steroids.
6. While the mix is playing, bypass the limiter and EQ plug-ins, listen, then turn them back on to hear the difference they added. Do you like what the plug-ins are adding, or not? Make adjustments accordingly. Keep flipping plug-ins on and off to hear the difference.

7. Next, un-solo this first track and solo up the next one. Try inserting the same plug-ins onto this track as the first one. Follow the same steps. Normally, before adding plug-ins, we'd take a listen to see what is needed, but since we are going for mass bulk overall, we'll go ahead and add plug-ins right away.

8. Next, begin to A/B this second, tweaked track with the first one. Listen to one for a moment, mute it, and quickly turn the second mix on. Go back and forth and see if these two mixes have a similar volume and sonic shape (highs, mids, lows). Make corrections to the second mix until it sounds similar to first one.

9. Now pull up the third mix and follow the same steps. A/B this third, tweaked mix to the first two. Follow steps until all mixes have similar loudness and sonic shape.

10. To finish, simply bounce each tweaked track to disc.

11. Serve with vanilla-bean ice cream, chocolate syrup, and sprinkles. Enjoy!

FINE DETAILS FOR PRINTING MIXES

Some mastering engineers suggest that by "bouncing" a mix down through the stereo bus to a hard drive, you are running the music through an additional step of digital processing, which can slightly diminish the final sheen of the mix. To avoid this extra process, they suggest instead of doing the traditional "bounce" method in your DAW, route all of your tracks in the session to an empty stereo audio track, then record all the music tracks to this stereo audio track. Once recorded, "export" this stereo track to your drive. This way, you bypass the extra step of processing required when "bouncing."

Some mastering engeineers feel that if you are going to do the traditional "bounce" route, print the mix as "left and right mono tracks" instead of using the "interlaced" option provided by most professional DAWs. It is said that by asking the DAW to conveniently "glue" the left and right channels together by choosing "interlacing" when bouncing, you are again running your music through an additional step of processing, thus diminishing your mix a tiny bit.

So there you go… some fine points to consider. But at the end of the day, if you're still cutting your teeth on your mix skills, don't worry about these details now. Bottom line, if a little girl can hum your melody, or a dude is head-banding to your song because it rocks, then you're winning!

Keep it all in perspective.

CHAPTER 13
THINGS TO CONSIDER WHEN ENTERING THE MUSIC BUSINESS

1. Determine who you are.
- Producer
- Songwriter
- Beat maker
- Mixer
- Post-production person
- Mastering engineer
- Manager/agent/promo person
- Combination of these

Ultimately, build your "reel," at least three pieces that show your work.

2. What is your goal, if it is to be an artist?
- Make a living as an independent artist.
    - *Sell less product, but make the lion's share.*
- Attract a major label/company.
    - *iTunes hits, social media traffic, YouTube views*

3. Find out what your strong point is.
- Build your team from there.
- Find folks who do the "other stuff" better than you.

4. Stay up on the latest info on the music business.
- In between old industry model and new, so you must employ strategies to utilize best of both.
- The industry is changing every three to six months with the pace of technology.

5. Remember, there are no more demos.
- Everyone has a professional music production program now. There's too much competition.

- Your material must be 100 percent complete.

    If you have to make a disclaimer before playing your music, then it is not yet ready.

6. Keep your songs short and sweet.

- Don't give your listener too long of a song to listen to.

    We as humans want what we don't have, and don't want what we do have.

- No intros, no double sections, no fade-outs.

7. Get proficient at your equipment and your overall methods of execution.

It is important to have a system of doing things and folks in place to work with you.

- Recording
- Writing
- Recruiting
- Mixing
- Mastering/editing
- Promoting/marketing

8. Begin to build a Rolodex of contacts.

Collect business cards and make meaningful connections when out. Avoid fluff conversations and engage with sincere folks. Filter through the fluff.

- Musicians/creative folks
- Beat makers
- Executives
- Street marketers
- And so forth

9. Make your package bigger than just music.

You must tie in "lifestyle" material. For example:

- A video that perfectly complements current music you are featuring
- Personal videos
- Odd antics
- Merchandise, etc.

10. Seek advice.

Get as many objective opinions as you can regarding your music.

- 5–10 music professionals
- 10–20 peers
- 20–40 random opinions from laymen

    See what the consensus says and be honest with yourself. Re-tool if necessary.

11. Recruit interns as worker bees.
- Organize and motivate enthusiastic, young energy to do marketing, blogging, busy work.
- Recruit from high schools, colleges, concerts, etc.

12. Put yourself in front of folks who matter.
- There are two degrees of separation between everyone in the music industry.
- Do research on those you want to meet.
- Target individuals.

13. Network, network, network!
- ASCAP, BMI, and SESAC are always hosting social events.

14. Merchandise means additional reach for your product.
- Contract out to create and/or sell.
- Do it yourself.

15. Sell your product and merchandise at shows.
- Once again, it depends on what your goals are.
- Are you trying to stay independent or attract a major company?

16. Make shows count.
Don't play gigs just for the sake of playing. Make sure you have an ulterior motive for gigging.
- You want to direct eyeballs to your product or site.
- You want to sell product and/or merchandise.
- You want to build your mailing list.
- You want to hold a showcase for folks that count.

APPENDIX
EMAIL CORRESPONDENCE

Over the years, I've answered many questions through email from students on a wide range of topics. What follows here are just a few.

QUESTION
Hey Darryl,

I need words from a wise. A friend wants to record vocals with me, eight songs total, mixing and mastering (in the box). Sounds cool, but he has no budget. Should I work on spec? How does that work? Is that a written agreement about the time I spent doing his project and if he makes money he has to pay my time? Or should I not charge as always and keep waiting for the next thing? What do you think? Thanks, man.

–Marty

ANSWER
Hi Marty,

First of all, if doing this project does not take away from you making money somewhere else, then yes, do it.
Reasons for doing it:

1. You get to sharpen your skills even more in a real setting.
2. You have the possibility of getting some benefit if something does happen with the project.
3. You get the credit, and get to build your producer/engineer/mixer reel, which is always a work-in-progress.
4. You never know what folks you'll meet on the journey. I've received so many unexpected benefits from just being in my craft.

Keep track of the hours you put in to the project, and the tasks you perform. You can draft a simple agreement stating that if he does receive a budget or some benefit from the finished product you create together, then:

1. You get a percentage of the total amount he receives (maybe 5–10 percent) or…
2. You get paid a flat rate (maybe $1,000–$5,000). Estimate how many hours it will take to complete the project, then multiply that by $50/hour. That will give you a reasonable number to base things on.

Also, you might say that you will require him to pay you a small chunk of money each month, maybe $150–$300, as a good-faith gesture on his part. If he really believes in himself, he can cough up few hundred bucks for you. That is not hard to do.

Okay man, marinate on this for now and hit me again if you need more feedback. Always stay in a project or two – or three. Stay busy making music!

–Darryl

COMMENTS

Great stuff. You have the goods, you just need product and a plan of action. A former boss once taught me a great phrase: Plan your work, then work your plan.

Yeah, this new year it's time to kick some butt, kick in some doors like the mafia, and take no crap from anyone. No more Mr. Nice Guy, because that guy always finishes last. I've learned that the hard way.

We want single-mindedness on the objective, yet always to stay aware of our surroundings and opportunities. We won't let any unsolicited, outside influence obstruct or distract us from achieving the goal. And the goal is: achieving each step one after another on our list.

I used to find myself getting distracted from my goals all the time by taking in too much other media: too many movies, being a fan of others' projects, reading too many creative billboards while driving, grazing too many articles on others who were winning, surfing YouTube too much, etc. It eventually begins to spin your head and you forget what is special about your own goals. Staying in your lane and not worrying about everyone else's projects is essential.

We are Content Creators, not Consumers anymore. God bless consumers. They buy our products and offerings. We need them, but we are not one of them anymore.

Creating the product is the easy part. You set ambitious yet achievable goals for the enterprise, then chart out how to hit these marks. That's where the true success of a company lies. Set your goals in increments:

- 6 months
- 1 year
- 18 months
- 2 years
- 5 years

If you want to make it in the music business, you have to look at this endeavor as a company, not some little side thing. Everyone and their mother is making cool music, but 99 percent of them end up just bumping their music for their boys. That's cool – but hey, if you are going to take the time to raise capital, then be that one percent who approaches it as a professional structure/undertaking. Think strategically and create trackable success – something that you can parlay into a major asset down the road.

It is all about building your brand. Vaseline®. Band-Aid®. Microsoft. Apple. That's the way one has to think. When you build the brand, the music becomes the marketing tool of building your brand.

QUESTION
Darryl,

I'm in love with this tune, but can't get the rights from the guy. I asked Larry if he wanted to re-do the production for me, but if you – or someone you know – are interested, please let me know.

Thanks again,

–Seth

ANSWER
Seth,

Tell the guy you're going to do a 50/50 split with him and release the song. Inform him you are not using his track "exclusively," meaning he can place it on someone else if he wants. That way, he has nothing to lose.

Once your song blows up and a publisher or distributor wants to get involved, then he may have to grant exclusivity. He will have no problem at that point, since there will be money on the table. Let him know that's the deal and that he has nothing to lose and everything to gain.

–Darryl

QUESTION
Darryl,

My name is T. I was in Dett Auditorium at the university on Thursday morning when you spoke to us. I am the one who told you I am an aspiring R&B/soul artist who wants to live in L.A.

I record and write my own lyrics, and most of the music comes out of my head as well, unless I ask my buddy Matt to help me produce a beat because I can't get the sound I want. I put my songs on SoundCloud and YouTube and promote links to my newest songs. I also spend a lot of my time doing covers and singing at open mics. I don't really consider myself a producer, because, like I said before, I often get help, but almost everything I write, I come up with the chords as well, just by sitting at a piano and finding what sound I want.

I am seeking your guidance and advice. I am a graduating senior, and my plans after graduation are not really finalized, but I'm thinking I want to move to L.A. and find an engineering/sound job in TV, radio, or movies and/or work sound at live concerts and events to fund my passion, which is singing, songwriting, and collaboration with other artists and producers.

I was born and raised in Virginia, and have lived here all my life. I feel as though staying here will not be conducive to my success, given my aspirations. New York and Atlanta are also ideas others have suggested as places to move, but I really want to move to L.A. Please advise! Thank you for your attention.

 −T

ANSWER

Hey T,

I remember you. Good to hear from you. I feel you on your thoughts. L.A., New York City, and Atlanta – yes indeed, all possibilities – but I feel your instincts are on point in wanting to move to L.A. L.A. is where the music biz truly is.

NYC is dope and lots of venues and clubs to play and work at, but the cost of living and the weather is so wrong in NYC. I swear, one really has to have a deep love and passion for NYC, because it is an unforgiving city. ATL is cool, but it's like *this* big. (I just snapped my finger). L.A. is cool and the cost of living is not nearly as high as NYC. There are tons of clubs you can do sound at as well, plus the overall energy is chill. L.A. has its own pace.

One suggestion/idea is to come out to L.A. for a few years and get put up on true game, then go back to Virginia and run things. Once you absorb the energy of where all media evolves from, your perspective widens. Then you take that knowledge back to where folks are moving at half-speed, set up shop, and dominate.

There are lots of folks out here, which is great, but it also creates huge competition. But if you take the L.A. education back to unpopulated media spots, you can really plant your flag and stand out where folks are moving slow.

Regarding doing sound, there are many opportunities to start as an intern at a club, then move into a "house" sound person.

I suggest you come out with at least six months of expenses so you can find a cool place to live and find a cool day gig until you land a job in your field, all the while collabing and working on your music. There is no shortage of musicians, producers, and songwriters to work with. And if you ever did come out, I'd show you around to get you acclimated to what's what.

Okay, chew on all this for a bit and feel free to hit me back for any clarity.
Talk later,

 −Darryl

COMMENTS

I'm happy to chat with him and help oversee his development as an artist. His songs are strong enough to stand on their own, but adding production (building the songs out with more musical layers and tones) would sell them much better. For now, though, he needs to continue to write constantly and keep performing.

It would be instructive for him to perform his songs with different combinations of musicians, in addition to his buddy Matt. Add drums, cello, an organ, accordion, tabla, bagpipes, a synth person to tack on different sounds to the mix. There are no rules to creativity; he should seek out every creative person he can and be his own talent scout. It's fun!

But he obviously needs to do a few rehearsals prior to each gig with whatever combos of players are going to play at the gig. He does not need to form an official band, just rotate different players every few gigs. Try new combos. This exercise of him scouting all types of players and rehearsing them is going to widen his scope as a songwriter and a performer. It will develop his producer skills as well. The various musicians will have an influence on him and grow his craft exponentially. This should be a steady exercise for him.

Also, when he is ready to record and develop his first produced, professional body of work, he will be up to speed with the arrangements of each song – what instrument plays what part at what time – as opposed to relying on the producer to figure it out. It will happen through osmosis by constantly rehearsing, growing, and performing with different types of players and the styles each player brings to the fold.

A FEW MORE COMMENTS

Here are six points for creating better odds for success in the entertainment industry:

- Goals: Stay on track with your goals. Be aware of new trends, but don't be swayed by every one that surfaces. Plan your work, then work your plan. Chip away at it daily. Stay in your craft. Meet new people all the time. Always look for opportunity wormholes; explore every opportunity that surfaces, but stay on track with your primary objectives.
- Flexibility: Be able to adapt and multi-task in whatever way needed. There is a fine line between staying on track and knowing when to adjust your roll or direction.
- Objectivity: Have the ability to be truly honest with yourself. Solicit feedback and keep your ego in check enough to apply constructive points.
- Instincts: Learn to trust you heart. Know when to go with your gut or change direction.
- Talent: This applies to more than just creative talent. Know what your true strong points are and apply them. Do what you know, and learn what you don't know.
- Collaborate: Bring in/work with others who can push your goals forward. Partner with people who share a common goal.

QUESTION

Hey Darryl,

I hope all is well with you. Do you know of any engineer or assistant engineer gigs out there? It can be studio and or live sound. I'm looking for more work.

Thanks,

–Jesse

ANSWER

Hey Jesse,

There are thousands of clubs in L.A. They're always looking for live sound engineers. These jobs may not pay the most, but least you are in your craft and making a few dollars steadily. (Btw, I've come across a handful of former students who run sound at various clubs around town.)

Get an L.A. *Weekly* magazine and list every club you see (club listings are about 3/4 way back into the paper), then put together a tight résumé and get it to all the clubs. Make sure your résumé states that you understand live sound, which is a different beast than studio recording, because live sound is spontaneous! You may want to visit many of these clubs during evening club hours and speak directly with whatever soundman is working. That way, you'll get the real 411 from him as to who to holler at.

Have you thought of possibly doing "post work" as well? It's harder to get into, but it's way more money.

Holler,

–Darryl

QUESTION

Hey Darryl,

I've been writing my music and I have most of lyrics copy written. How do I go about selling my lyrics or working toward that route?

Thanks,

–Janeen

ANSWER

Hi Janeen,

Regarding selling your lyrics, there are a few avenues. One is a publishing deal, when you join forces with a music publisher. Think of them as a song pimp. They get your songs placed in commercials, with other artists, etc.

In order to get a publishing deal, it is best if your lyrics are first married to a melody. Most publishers want to hear the melody and how it fits with the accompaniment (chords, etc.); they don't have the vision to hear/see only lyrics, since everyone has a DAW (digital audio workstation; Pro Tools, Logic, Ableton, GarageBand, Reason, et al) and is turning in professional-sounding material.

It's good if you can find a music person/track cat who needs lyrics put on his tracks, so the two of you collaborate. It is a win-win deal, because he needs lyrics/melody to complete his bare tracks, and you need a bed for your lyrics to marry to. With a DAW, they have the ability to record your voice as well.

You do not have to pay them. Any cat that says you need to pay is full of it. When you are collabing/co-writing with someone, both of you are contributing equally to the equation. It is in his best interest to want to record your vocals on his track because you complete each other. Both of you come out with a complete song, as opposed to you having only lyrics, and him having only a track.

Look on Craigslist for music programmers. You could also place an ad yourself looking for beat makers who want to collab with you. Ask every musical person you know if they know any beat makers. Track cats are abundant. Lyricists like yourself are hard to find, so most will be happy to work with you. Don't let any of them run game on you. What I'm telling you here is the real deal.

Once you begin to write with a cat, don't stop looking for more cats, because the more folks you write with, the more your name will circulate and the more folks will start searching you out for your lyrics, and to create/sing hooks on tracks.

You also must create a web presence for yourself (website, Facebook, etc.). Here you will place all the songs you have collaborated on. It is how folks (potential writers, etc.) can check you out.

Once you have a body of work (6–8 full songs; your lyrics, melodies, and accompaniment) that you are proud of, then you can begin to scout out music publishers for a possible publishing deal. In another email, we'll discuss how to protect your lyrics when collabing with others. This is more than enough info for you to get rolling for now. Please let me know you received this email.

Thanks, Janeen!

–Darryl

A DIALOGUE

Hey Darryl,

Tonight I was at Whole Foods and I ran into Nigel from B**** band. He was there with his girlfriend. I went and introduced myself and told him I just got out here and that I was a songwriter and I was wondering if he could spare ten minutes of his time to talk to me and mentor me. He goes, "Yeah sure, take my email." What do you think I should do? Should I email him or do you think he was just trying to be nice and will never reply to my email. If I write, what should I say to him?

–Becca

Hey Becca,

You should email him for sure. Absolutely. Email him either now or in the morning and in the subject window put "Producer girl you met in Whole Foods."

Then write a brief email that says, "Hey there, I met you in Whole Foods Wednesday evening. Thanks for your email address. I would love it if we could have a brief creative chat or email dialogue. Thanks so much." Then when you have the real conversation with him, ask if you could apprentice under him for a short time. Go for it! Keep your email brief and to the point, only three or four sentences. God bless.

–Darryl

Okay, cool. I'll do that in the morning. I also gave him my card when he gave me his email. Hey, thanks so much.

My pleasure. Good for you for seizing an opportunity spontaneously.

Actually I almost did not do it, but at the end I forced myself. The worst that could have happened was that he would be a jerk. But he was really cool. I hope it wasn't just to be polite.

That's right. Good thinking. Hey, you gave it your best shot either way. You are training yourself to seize opportunities whenever they appear. You have already won.

QUESTION

Hey Darryl,

I am looking to find people that write and compose. Do you know where to go to find people to do this? I know it's probably going to cost a pretty penny to get this done, and I don't have a lot of money right now. Still, I want to do this, even if it's one song at a time because I know myself. I can't get anywhere just doing covers forever. Thanks for your reply,

–Shana

ANSWER

Hi Shana,

You are correct: Cover songs will go only so far. There are a few options on how to find songs to perform. First of all, if you have a passion and desire to write or co-write your own material, I suggest you start by finding songwriters and asking them if they have any tunes that are maybe 80 percent complete. Ask if you can help finish the song with them.

Where do you find songwriters? Craigslist and Facebook are great places to begin and find folks who want their song performed. Also, ASCAP, BMI, and SESAC always hold monthly networking functions around town. Trust me, there are many songwriters out there who do not aspire to be an artist like you, but only want to write songs for artists to perform – kind of like a fashion designer needs a model to walk the runway at a fashion show and display their work. You know?

Get on Craigslist and place an ad saying you are a singer and are looking for songs to perform. Beef up who you are a little bit by saying you are putting a record together and are now scouting for a particular style of song. Describe what kind of songs you want, what kind of themes you want to sing about, and the general musical style you're looking for (up-tempo or ballads, mainstream, underground, or more theatrical, etc.).

Understand that there is a difference between the song itself and the production you wrap around the song. The song is the chord changes and the lyrics and melodies you sing. The production is the style you take the song in. Let's use "Mary Had a Little Lamb" as an example: The "song" is what your mother taught you as a kid, but the "production" is whether you fashion it for a punk band, a country singer, or a hip-hop artist.

Think about it: If a punk band recorded "Mary Had a Little Lamb," the drums would be hard-hitting and fast, the guitars would be aggressive, and the singer would be belting the lyrics (even though they're about a little girl and a nice little lamb). On the other hand, if a country artist were singing the song, there might be slide guitar, a soft beat, and a Southern-drawl vocal performance. It is still the same song, but it is performed in different ways and with different instrument sounds and styles.

Here's the point: You can receive a tune from a songwriter, and even though it may not sound like the kind of style you want to do, the song can be stripped down to its lyrics and melody, and new clothes can be wrapped around it to make it the style you want it to be. You will need a producer to do this for you. On the other hand, you may find a tune that is a good "song" (lyrics and melody) and is already laid down in the style you like. Sometimes you get lucky and are sent a song that already has the right clothing wrapped around it!

You still need a producer to assist you in recording your vocals on top of the accompaniment, though, unless you feel confident that you can get a great vocal performance on your own. Then you need to mix the song down so all the levels sound great before you burn it to CD and start distributing the product.

–Darryl

QUESTION

Hi Darryl,

Currently I do not play any musical instruments. I was learning guitar but my teacher moved to Thailand on a whim and I have not been able to afford what others are charging. I have been told that it is a must to have my own band or be part of a band or at least play some instrument.

I have been told by others that there are many vocalists out there who don't have a band, nor do they play any instrument. They instead have random bands that rotate in an out. Do I really need a band, or can I do it without one?

Thanks,

–Kyle

ANSWER

Hey Kyle,

It all depends on how you want to project yourself as an artist. Man, you could perform with a backing-track CD! You could use a laptop onstage and trigger your music on your own and perform your show. But if it is just you onstage alone, you will need to have lots of cool props and stage antics to keep the audience entertained. Be creative. For example, you may want to use your laptop and have a percussion player embellish the beat. For a different gig, you may want your laptop and a horn section. You get it? You can mix and match depending on the kind of show you're doing. This keeps it fun and spontaneous.

Right now, though, you don't need to focus on whether or not you need a band. If you create a buzz about your project, finding people to play for you will be easier than you might think. Get something happening around your project, and musicians will be knocking on your door to be a part of it. Musicians are plentiful! Trying to keep together a band of dedicated musicians is a job in itself. You probably would want to just hire musicians as you need them.

–Darryl

A FINANCIER – A DIALOGUE

Hi Darryl,

I was told to look for a financier. I guess there are some people or groups out there that might pick me up, again because of my voice and who would in turn get music written for me, get me polished up, etc., in exchange for a percent of the profit. To be honest, I'm not clear as to exactly what a financer is.

Thanks for your help,

–Hal

Hello Hal,

A financier is a person who might invest in you as an artist, financially speaking. They would have to believe in you, of course. Usually, you have to prove yourself by creating a buzz on your own before anyone will want to put money into your project. Most money folks first want to see that you have done your homework and that there is a market for your project; they want their investment to be safe and profitable.

Usually the first investors for most artists are their family members. You do not need a lot of money to get your project off the ground. You do not have to pay a songwriter to use their song. They own the song even though you are performing it. If you sell a CD, you then pay the songwriter a small fee called a "mechanical royalty." This is something like 9.1 cents each time you make a sale.

–Darryl

I was thinking the X Factor TV show might be what was meant by a financier. I went and auditioned. It started out with 18,000 and I made it through all three rounds to land in the final 300. One of the producers, who were not supposed to give any feedback, told me she thought I was fantastic. I am kind of let down this week because the show taping is a few days away and I was supposed to get a call back, but haven't yet. I think that ship has sailed, though I still got my round advance tickets.

So is a financier like a TV show or something? Or are there really people out there who do as described above if I sign my soul away? (Hey, I am willing to do it.) If there are people like that, do you have any tips on how to track them down?

First things first, Hal. Create some product – at least three songs that represent what you are trying to do. If someone were to play these three songs without knowing anything about you, they would completely represent you as an artist. You must first define your sound before anyone is going to put any money into you. It is up to you to take this first step. Period.

You will need a little money for a producer to help you put these initial three songs together, somewhere between $300–$1500 total. On the other hand, if you find a producer who believes in you, he'll do it on "spec" (meaning speculation); in other words, he will donate his time, hoping you will become a success and he will then get paid bigger down the road instead of making just a small fee now.

WHICH COMES FIRST, A CD OR STAGE PERFORMANCE? – A DIALOGUE

Hi Darryl,

I thought it would be best to start out by getting songs made for a CD or put onto iTunes so that people would get to know me. My music would be out somewhere before I did any performance. I mean, how are you going to get a crowd if no one knows who is going to be onstage?

But I have been told that I should be focusing on doing the performance part first, then after I have done that for a while, do a CD or something of the sort. So who is right here? I can't wrap my head around how it would be best to perform first, since no one would know who I am.

Thanks for your advice,

–Eric

Eric,

Listen to me: Create the CD first – unless you form a band and choose to create songs as a band and work on them over time. But that is a more haphazard way of approaching it. Find a producer and/or a songwriter who can help you create a body of work with/for you, then go from there. You must define the music before you can start performing it.

Holler,

–Darryl

I know this is a lot of stuff, and that not everything is in your area of expertise, but I just laid it out in case you might see something that you can answer. If you have anything to add for someone just starting, that would be awesome. I am not expecting to become a superstar overnight; in fact, I don't ever expect to be on superstar level, but I hope for at least indie star level somehow.

I still have learning to do. I still have vocal lessons and I am still looking at other ways to advance myself, including possible Musicians Institute attendance. I know I am kind of old to be a new rock star, but I am not kicking myself for not starting earlier. My mom was sick from the time I was 17 years old. I stayed home and took care of her until she passed away two years ago. It was at that point that my new life started and a friend found my voice by accident at a party.

Sure, I might not have a long career ahead of me. I might not even have any career, but I don't feel old and I am ready to go. I am ready to do it, even if it turns out to be a dead end. At least I'll be able to think back and know I gave it a try, instead of regretting – when I really am an old man – not doing anything

On a side note: How do I go about arranging a tour of Musicians Institute?

To find the date of the next open house, just go to the website (www.mi.edu). They are held regularly.

My vocal coach has told me she thinks it would be an excellent idea to take a tour. She went to MI and would be willing to go with me on the tour. How much advance notice should I give? I am seriously thinking about it. Maybe not right now, but a few months down the line.

Listen, Eric, I just finished a small book. I've attached it here. Please enjoy it. I know it will help you tremendously. Holler if you need any more info. Believe in yourself! You deserve goodness, man.

Once again, thank you very much for your time. I really do appreciate it. Who knows, maybe someday when I make it, I'll hire you to produce an album for me.

CONTRACTS – A DIALOGUE

Hi Darryl,

I hope all is well with you. I have a question. I'm writing a contract for Daniel, who is producing my song. What counts as co-producing? I wrote the melody, lyrics, and chord chart. We re-recorded some stuff, plus he added a whole bunch to the production of the music. Has he then co-produced it or has he produced it.

Thanks,

–Rachel

Hey Rachel,

Did he go into this as a producer? Did he contribute to the overall "sound" of the production, or dig through amp sounds or computer keyboard files to discover cool sounds, and/or prompt someone to perform any parts in a certain way? If he performed parts that contribute to the overall identity of the production, then yes, he could be considered a co-producer.

–Darryl

So I'm paying him for producing it, plus I want to add four percent producer royalties in the contract. Do I write it as a "work for hire"? Or what is it really called? What kind of royalties do I pay him – record sales, digital, or what's the most common thing? I'm all confused when it comes to this.

You are giving him a four percent producer royalty. His four percent comes from the actual sale of a physical song (or download). He does not get paid from the song being performed on the radio, etc. Only the songwriter gets that money from their PRO (performance rights organization; ASCAP, BMI, SECAC, et al).

Because he will share in the back-end royalties, it is not a "work for hire." A work for hire contract means he goes away after his services are rendered and never participates in any royalties. You can find a typical producer contract on the Internet. If you need a sample for reference, I can send you one I've signed in the past. Let me know.

I don't know if you mix for students, but I'm asking anyway. How much would you charge to mix a song?

Ha! How much do you have? Sure, I mix for folks. I don't see you as a student; I see you as a peer. Dating a female student is frowned upon by UCLA, but not working professionally. We are now and always will be musical allies. Holler at me about what you need mix-wise.

Let me know if you need any more clarity. I'm happy to holler at you.

QUESTION

Hey Darryl!

I just wrote a new song I'm really excited about! Also, what is the next step I should do pre-production-wise: pencil sketches, lead sheets, rough recordings, etc.?

–Jake

ANSWER

Hey Jake,

It's always great to hear when a songwriter comes up with an inspired new song. I'd love to hear it. Email it over when you rough-record it down. I never care how raw the recording is; I can hear past low recording quality and average performance. I can hear the essence of the song itself.

But, as I'm sure you know, most folks cannot hear past raw – or lack of – production value; they take what they hear at face value. If it sounds shiny and polished, most think it is good, even if the song itself stinks. Same goes in reverse: great song, but no production; they think it is incomplete or not dope. The moral of the story: Be careful who you play your rough demos for. I'm sure you already understand that, though.

Regarding next steps for pre-production, sure man. I'll create a detailed email of bullet points on how to go about pre-pro, then we can get on the phone again and go through them. Cool?

Holler back,

—DSwann

QUESTION

Hi Darryl!

This is Alex from your UCLA producing class. I hope you've been well. I refer to my notes from your class on a regular basis, so thank you so much for all the golden nuggets of knowledge and the Magic Frequencies!

I'd like to ask you a question about the RME Fireface interfaces. I am interested in the Fireface 800 and 400 and people have told me that they both have excellent internal preamps. Do you have experience with RME's interfaces?

If so, my question is this: Is the quality of the Fireface preamps good enough that I could get professional recordings without an additional external preamp? Or do you think I need another external preamp to get professional results?

Right now I am recording mostly acoustic guitar and vocals, but I will eventually be recording electric guitars, bass, MIDI keyboards, MIDI drums, and possibly acoustic drums. The songs are in the indie/folk/alt country/rock pop categories (specific, I know).

Thanks so much!

—Alex

ANSWER

Alex,

This looks like a quality piece of gear, really clean and efficient. I have not had any experience with this box, but from what I've just read, it looks solid. Especially if you are doing acoustic guitars and vocals, this interface will deliver clean signal.

Now when you run heavy guitar amps and live kick-in snare drums through it, I'm not sure how it will stand up, but as long as you don't drive the mic-pre too hot, it looks like it will deliver clean signal.

Usually, with high-end mic-pres, you can drive the signal really hot, just before distortion, and get the warmest tone the pre can deliver. But if you were to try that with an inexpensive mic-pre, it would sound like crap and very tinny as you approach the higher levels of the pre.

In closing, this looks like a quality piece of gear! I hope this helps, man. Stop by class anytime to hang if you like: Room B-06 on Thursdays, 7–10 p.m.

—DSwann

COMMENTS

If you're only a casual camper, you are not a Navy Seal, but if you're a Navy Seal, you can always go casual camping. What does being a Navy Seal mean? Making some dope music, but also adhering to industry standards (to use the term lightly). What does this mean?

1. If there were a budget, could you deliver on budget?
2. If there is a time deadline, can you hit it while also delivering something dope?
3. Can the marketing department of the company truly market it? Does it have a lane out there in the jacked-up commercial industry?
4. Does the final product stand up next to the competition well if you were to A/B it against whatever is considered hot in the commercial world now?
5. Most importantly, do you – the producer and the artist – truly feel you've brought the production home? Do you stand behind it fully, or are you a little unsure of the final product?

Okay, so there you go, man. Just some things to think about and keep you pushing, but you're doing great, dude.

–Darryl

REPLY TO A QUESTION

Sorry for the delay hitting you back. Got real busy last few days over here.

Question: Have you ever created a production (or body of music) that is totally your vision, sound- and production-wise? Your creative brain-child? Or has everything you've done professionally incorporated band members' creative input as well?

If the answer is no, never done a pure Evelyn production, then next step is probably to do that. Hopefully this is going to be your next step regardless, a true Evelyn production. Then as I said, musicians learn their "parts" from the record. It's the very best way to create a rock-solid foundation for a project.

What steps have you taken to "shop" your project to labels, or what steps have you taken to bring awareness to your project? Can you bullet-point them in chronological order?

ANSWER

It seems like you need some definitive goal-setting, then a comprehensive plan of action to achieve the goal. Attached is a "Who's Looking List" I receive from a publisher every month. These lists help their writers zero in on artists who are looking for songs that the music publisher can pitch to.

But this list also doubles as a Rosetta Stone of the pop music industry. It shows every A&R person in position now, who they signed recently, and what the artist is like and coming out with creatively.

Marinate on this list and gather intel on what's happening in the biz. Look for A&R folks who are signing interesting artists, not the typical cookie-cutter stuff. Research the artists, research the A&R folks, Google them and get some backstory.

In my opinion, you need:

1. Three to five songs that represent you well and also have enough edge and relativity to be relevant to A&R ears.
2. An awareness campaign. I have attached a cool sheet on strategic awareness: "Grass Roots Promotion Tips." Just replace your name in place of project name, "sPYrADIO." Also I've attached a cool link on branding a project or artist.
3. A band that can pull off a dope showcase for industry. Remember, a "band" does not always have to be the typical line-up of drums, bass, guitar, etc. There are many ways to push the envelope these days by mashing together interesting live elements: DJs, sample-dudes, percussionists, players that perform on several instruments and each player has a workstation in addition to his regular instrument.
4. A small, dedicated team of bloggers and social-networkers to pump your brand.
5. Once some awareness is built, begin opening for some name artists. You have the goods to attract a booking agent.
6. Establish a residency at a club weekly or biweekly for a period of time.
7. Once some of these are exercised, set up an industry showcase for your project. Your PRO (ASCAP) can be helpful with this, especially if you are already making some good noise with the above points.

Marinate on this for a bit and hit me back if you want to continue the dialogue.

ANSWER

Hey Jake,

Let's carve out some main points for how to move forward with the pre-production process:

Step 1: Due Diligence

The first step is to have a few creative discussions with your producer. (I'm happy to serve in this role for you as much as I can, if you like.)

Some questions I ask artists are:

1. *If you were playing at a huge arena tomorrow night, what would you wear?* Literally. Shoes, pants, top? What would you do with your hair? It may sound silly, but the music production/sound must match the artist's physical image. (Jake, I know you are a chill dude and probably enjoy rocking the scaled-down look onstage because it's all about the music for you, as most true artists feel. But it is important that you now begin to think about image. You must have a "look," even if your look appears

like you don't have a look. It must be conscious, because having the non-look look is a thought-out image in itself.)

Artists and bands that look like they don't care about image truly have thought the look through and usually have a stylist that makes them look like they don't give a darn about their image. The irony of showbiz is that it's all perception to make the consumer believe what they want the consumer to believe. Welcome to Hollywood!

2. *What would your stage set-up be?* If I were sitting in the audience, what would be the positions onstage, and the instrumentation of your "in a perfect world" band? Think of your ultimate band. Spare no expense. Think this through and take your time in creating this in your head.

For example: Do you want to have two long-haired dudes with guitars hanging real low on both sides of you, or do you perhaps see a horn section on stage left. Do you see a small string section next to the drummer, or up front stage right? Drums and percussion? A DJ with a drummer? A few really hot girls as backup singers? Dudes as singers?

The sky is the limit, so create your ideal band, instrument by instrument, and where they will be onstage.

Trust me, man, indulge me in this mental exercise. The reason is two-fold: 1) It helps producer determine what kinds of musical elements you hear in your music; 2) It helps initiate the manifestation of your ultimate goal and sets your thinking on a much larger scale. It gives you a much wider perspective of your career than what you have experienced so far – which typically is you soloing on a keyboard, playing live on a bare stage. (There's nothing wrong with that! It's the perfect place for you to be so far!)

3. *Let's make a sonic sandwich:*
   a. If you could have anyone's drums, whose would they be? You could say you'd like to have a mix between James Brown drums (tight and funky pocket), and old school Elton John drums (lots of movement, understated playing, loose groove, moves with all the transitions of the chords).
   b. If you could have anyone's musical layers, whose would that be? You might say Radiohead (ambient, atmospheric, very musical, arpeggiated chords, and random eclectic elements).
   c. If you could have anyone's background vocals, whose would they be? Maybe you'd say old school Aretha Franklin ("doo-doo'" soul-sista sound), or you may say pop band MGMT (retro-pop backgrounds, as in the song "Trees" – lots of layers and a polished sound).
   d. If your lead vocals could come off like anyone's, whose would they be like? You may say like James Taylor (easy-listening, lyrical, and smooth) or you may say Joe Cocker (passionate, deeply emotional, lots of moaning and bleeding). For vocals, I mean the delivery. You sing well and have solid pitch, but your style/

delivery/performance needs to be developed further. You sing in your comfort zone, which is perfectly fine, but I know there is lots more horsepower there. You need to be pushed in the studio to tap into the undiscovered tones and styles in you. This is all part of your artist development. Think about these.

Step 2: Song Selection

First, you must determine how many songs you want your final product to have. Ideally, there should be twice the number of songs to choose from. For example, if you want to deliver a seven-song EP, then you need ten to 14 songs; a five-song EP needs eight to ten songs to select from, etc. It's kind of like a gene pool – better to have more and diverse genes available to create the healthiest baby. These songs can be in any shape – rough recordings, however you have them – as long as the producer can hear the song clearly, with no stops or mistakes.

Obviously, it's best to go through the batch of candidate songs with your producer or someone who understands your ultimate goal, both production-wise and music-wise. You and the producer each pick nine favorites out of this batch of 14 or 15. Each of you should take a few days to objectively pick your nine songs. (Nine, because you are narrowing these down from the big batch of 14, but two more will eventually be cut. It's good to chew on nine, then see which seven remain after the acid test that follows.)

Next, have a little creative discussion; each of you lays his cards on the table. You both will have picked many of the same songs, but the ones that are different can be discussed and creatively debated. "Why should this one or that one be picked?"

Then the producer throws battery acid on these nine and sees which two dissolve, leaving the final seven. By battery acid, we mean the producer marinates on the songs, determining the quality of:

- Lyrics
- Melodies
- Song structure
- Tempo
- Key

The producer pulls and tugs at the songs in his/her DAW, using the above criteria. (I could go into explanation, but it's too much to write here. If you're curious, it's all in that book I sent.)

Step 3: Chop up ideas in ProTools.

In this step, the producer begins to play with sounds and layers in the DAW and to experiment with combinations of rhythms and chord tones. As variations are created, the producer emails the artist to see what vibes he (the artist) does and does not like. These are all pencil-sketch layers, rhythms, and sounds – just to find some footing.

Once the producer and artist go back and forth many times over a few weeks, a sound outline/blueprint begins to take shape for each song. Once a blueprint is achieved for all seven songs, this step is over.

Step 4: Determine plan of action for recording.
A production schedule is now created on how best to execute the different stages of recording.

Basic steps are:
1. Root tracking (drums, bass, piano; root instruments)
2. Overdubs (solos; vocals, lead and backing). Overdubs can require as many as eight to ten four-hour sessions.
3. Editing (tuning, tweaking flubs, chopping and moving sections of song around, etc.)
4. Mixing
5. Mastering

There are many approaches for this step. If you're dealing with a band, then there is a whole rehearsal regimen to go through before entering into the recording studio. If it is a solo artist, male or female, are there drum-machine elements to be used? Are there live musicians to be added after, or is the whole production going to take place "in the box"? (In other words, in the computer: Pro Tools, Logic, etc. Dance music, R&B, and pop – 90 percent is done in the box.)

If we're talking about a singer-songwriter like yourself, are there synthetic elements (e.g., a drum loop) that form the core of the production for a particular song? Do live instruments form the core?

Also, if you're using live musicians, each instrumentalist must be handpicked and rehearsed prior to taking them into the recording studio. If you don't do that, you will just be shooting in the dark and wasting money and studio time. Musicians must be determined by their:
- Skill
- Style needed for a particular element in a given song
- Access to gear and instruments
- Attitude
- Availability
- Cost
- And so forth

Once you marinate and absorb a little, we'll talk it through and move forward. See ya,
   –DSwann

COMMENTS

I hear you, Rose. Keep applying and applying! You are a survivor and you will have success because you have staying power. I respect that. I see lots of folks come and go, but you have a big heart and girth. You're going to find the perfect slot career-wise, I know it. In the meantime, you'll find whatever you need to stay afloat. Have you considered waitressing as a holdover? Also, have you applied at:

1. Music stores? Guitar Center (all locations), Sam Ash, West L.A. Music.
2. Recording studios? There are nearly 200 commercial studios in L.A. alone. Send a résumé to all of them.
3. Pro-audio gear-rental places? Audio Rents. You can speak to T and tell her I referred you. She is really sweet. Also SIR, etc., etc. There are nearly 80 music gear service businesses in Hollywood (rehearsal halls, showcase facilities, gear rental spots, gear transport companies like Leeds, Mates, et al.).
4. "Post" houses? There are probably 300 in Hollywood alone.

You are a smart, attractive, personable young woman – which is exactly what many of these places look for. Google all of these types of places and send your résumé to all of 'em! I'll shoot you more ideas as they come to me.

QUESTION
Hey Darryl,

I have a quick question. Are royalties and publishing two different things? For example, if I produce a track for an artist and they wrote the lyrics, but they aren't willing to give up any of their writer's share of publishing – but I request three percent of royalties on the song and or CD sales – that is two different things, right?
–Noel

ANSWER
Noel,

Yes indeed, publishing and producer royalties are two separate things. First of all, the word "royalty" simply means an earned percentage you are to receive. Royalties can mean producer royalties or publishing royalties, so it is important to distinguish which one an artist is speaking of when discussing; things can get confusing when speaking generally of royalties. But the whole "standard" royalty rate thing is changing due to the constantly changing music industry.

And yes, it is customary for a producer to get a three percent producer royalty. He gets paid a producer fee up front for working on the product, and if product does well and becomes a commercial success, then the producer gets to participate in the back-end winnings (royalties) as well.
–DSwann

QUESTION

Darryl,

I listened to the roughs of the mixes I gave you and I like them creatively a little better. Maybe it's just what I'm used to after laying down vocals, etc. Perhaps it would help if we work on them together. Does that help you more or do I just make you crazy?

–Jack

ANSWER

Jack,

No problem if you like your roughs better, creatively speaking. Totally understood. From a mixer perspective, your roughs are sonically loose. My job is to capture the spirit of your demos and at the same time make it sonically tight so it translates best on all listening devices.

There are underlying details that must be addressed sonically for a recording to stand up against the pro stuff out there in the marketplace. I'm sure your demos sound good to you for a couple of reasons: 1) You are used to hearing stuff on your system; 2) You are totally inside your creative world, which you should be.

It's all good, bro. I just want you to understand that there are issues a mixer must address and nail for a production to translate universally in the outside world. Let me play with your notes and shoot you another round, then we can dial in together after that.

–Darryl

RECORDING FEES – A DIALOGUE

Darryl,

I'm working with these kids. They spit over Kanye- and Drake-like beats, but we are currently working on original tracks. I'm charging an hourly rate, which has been cool. But the pops, who is paying, is somebody I want to keep happy. I played the dude some beats I've done and he was digging them. I'm wondering how to deal with the situation. Even with the original track we are doing, should I be charging hourly or charge by the track?

–Sean

Sean,

I usually charge by the song, not hourly. Then I charge another fee to mix when done. But I've been burned many times because the artist wants to keep adding vocals and re-doing vocals, then writing new verses, etc., etc. I end up doing way more "tracking" than what I charged for the flat fee for the song.

A flat fee is customary and shows the investor you are not trying to nickel and dime him by running up hours. It takes the pressure off you in that you can take as much time as you need to get the production right without having to constantly go back to an investor for more hourly money to get the performances you need.

But since you own your own studio, only your time is in question. If you were in someone else's studio, the hourly thing would really eat into an investor's pocket. Then again, keeping it hourly keeps the artist from going crazy with multiple overdubs and unnecessary re-dos, etc.

It also depends whether the artists are just having fun and spittin' on mic for the sake of "being on the mic" or if you guys are working toward completing X number of songs and have a specific goal to finish a body of work. If the former (having fun on mic), keep it hourly. If you are working toward a specific goal, then have a face to face with the investor (pops) and give him a few choices:

1. Stay on hourly rate until mix time.
2. Work out a flat rate per song until mix time.
3. Work out an all-inclusive song rate, with tracking and mixing included in the total cost.
4. Work out an all-inclusive rate for the entire project rate (tracking and mixing for all intended songs in total cost).
5. Do a flat rate up to X number of hours. If they exceed that number, start charging hourly. This system works well.

You will have to crunch some numbers to come up with these amounts. Doing a flat rate behooves you in that you get chunks of money: half when you begin, and half when you complete. It behooves the investor, too, in that he gets a slight break in overall expenditure and can project his funds by knowing the bottom-line cost.

To come up with a flat rate, estimate how many hours it will take to complete all necessary vocals, based on your past experience with these artists. Add another four to six hours for your personal vocal tuning and aligning, and production time – whatever your hourly production rate. ($50/hr is a good benchmark rate to use.) If you need additional help calculating these four scenarios, let me know.
Later,

   –Darryl

Obviously hourly brings in more cash, but I might lose a customer. I don't even know how much to sell beats for. If I were to charge, how much? Would I still be able to use a beat?

Remember, selling a beat is different than leasing a beat. If you sell a beat, that means you relinquish all ownership of your creation and give that ownership to the purchaser. If you're going to sell a beat, charge a nice chunk because you will not be allowed to use that beat again unless you get permission from new owner. Calculate the beat's potential for earning in its life with these new owners.

Take into consideration both mechanical royalties (in which the beat is placed on a CD and generates approximately ten cents for every CD sold), and performance royalties (when the beat is played on radio or any other public performance use).

Also consider digital purchases since CD sales have declined dramatically. At the end of the day, I'd charge $500–$2500 to sell the beat. If these were artists signed to a major distributor, that sell cost would go up dramatically since there is a bigger possibility that the beat will have a brighter life and higher earning potential. You will miss out on all the back-end earning of your creation if you sell, so you'd better get it up front.

It is customary for you to lease the beat to them; that way, you retain ownership. Remember: A song is divided up by 50 percent "music" and 50 percent lyrics and melody. If the other party writes all the lyrics and melodies, then the split (ownership) of song will be 50 percent for you (beat creator), and a 50 percent split between whoever wrote the lyrics and melodies. You can charge an investor an amount of money (maybe $250–$1000) so the beat stays exclusive for their use for, let's say, six months to a year.

Make it a sliding scale: the more they pay for the lease, the longer they have exclusive use (you won't put it on anyone else); for a lesser amount, they have a shorter exclusive use. Be sure to discuss all this up front with the investor; this will create trust and honor between you guys. And don't be a jerk like many folks are, getting exclusive-use money from the client, then pimping the track out to everyone and their brother.

Use your own good judgment. You can always play the beat for others. If they like it, you can create a derivative of the beat for new artist – just flip it a little different.

Think on these things. You know me: I could go on and on.

QUESTION
Hi Darryl,

I'm still with the band – getting ready to record a new batch of songs and having a bit of realization and conflict. I always envisioned the live show with a band, but being in a band isn't for me. I'm dealing with how to relay this to the guys. My latest puzzle, but I'm close to figuring it out.

–Evie

ANSWER
Hey Evie,

I hear you! Being in a band is so different. It is actual work. I always saw you as a solo artist with a band behind her – your vision, your sound. You have great instincts and all the charisma to be a solo artist. Define and produce your "sound" out fully in the studio, then the band learns the parts and plays it live.

Too many times there are too many different influences coming from too many members in a band, too many cooks in the kitchen and not every cook is a good cook. There are many great players, but not everyone has great creative ideas for parts and layers that fit into the grand scheme of what will create the best overall sound for the particular production. And sometimes their ego will not allow them to realize that they should just listen sometimes.

Feel free to bend my ear if you need to. I've been through it all. You're starting to go through it yourself.

–Darryl

QUESTION
Music Guru,

I've been reading that last email you sent me – the one about the "band" issues – every day since. I've been doing so much thinking. I am naturally a humble and quiet person. So far I sense all the people I've met think well of me, but it hasn't gotten me far enough. So, I'm about to do it. Be conceited. Ready?... I'm fantastic! I'm badass. I just haven't been in the right situation yet. I've been in good ones, but none have been able to give me the help I need to climb up. I have days, few and far between, where I'm on it like a business woman. But the artist starts needing to hide away and just create. I can't rely on help with money anymore. It sucks. Money is just stupid pieces of paper.

If you don't mind my asking, did you struggle this way? I know the struggle never ends. But, was there a day you can remember that started something better?

–Evie

ANSWER
Oh, my goodness, Evie. You're welcome! You said it, sister: Nice guys finish last. There is no frickin' reward for being overly polite and nice. I'm not saying one needs to be a jerk, but it's time to stop indulging everyone else's feelings and do what is best for you. You've touched a revelation nerve with me with your email. I feel you 1000 percent.

You are in the list of Top 10 dopest artists I've come across in my 25 years out here trudging through these streets. That's real talk, E. It is 2 a.m. now. I was checking my email for the night and saw your message and had to say something to you. My trigger fingers (typing fingers) are itching to blaze a full-page reply this second, but let me marinate over the eve and reply tomorrow, because I want to give you all my attention. You deserve it.

God bless you, Comrade-sister. Yes, it does all happen in one moment. There is a tipping point and the next thing you know, a wormhole opens up for you and your life is never the same again. This is what happens as long as one stays in their craft – stays in their craft daily. Say yes to every opportunity until you have to say no; this way, your name spreads exponentially and before you know it, your name begins doubling back where it becomes synonymous with what's happening in town.

We can meet and have coffee one day and talk if you like. I could go on and on, but will continue tomorrow. You have "it," E. I know you know, but I'm confirming that it is very plain to see in you. It is only a matter of time and constant exploration of your craft for you. Promise.

Holler, and I'll write more.

–DS

PUBLISHING – A DIALOGUE

Darryl,

Quick question: Is it wise to put a watermark (like saying "Blah Blah Productions" throughout the whole song) on my music when I'm sending it publishers, music supervisors, labels, etc.?

–Josh

Hey Josh,

Tag it at the top and maybe at the end only. It is annoying to me when I hear it throughout whole song. A watermark is used for two reasons, as you know:

1. It lets the listener know who created what they are listening to.
2. It provides protection in case someone tries to "sample" a piece of your song.

If you are sending material to reputable contacts (professional companies) and have some type of rapport with them, even in the smallest way, most likely they are not going to rip your material. Have a solid cover letter (email) with the song as well. Keep it grindin'. Big ups, Josh!

–Darryl

This is of course the first thing I'll be publishing ever. I plan on signing up with one of the PROs and going to any kind of seminars/events available in the area and cultivating a contact there if I can. Beyond doing everything they recommend to move forward, is there anything I can add – on top of this publishing – to further legitimize what I'm trying to do?

As far as legitimizing yourself, you can affiliate with certain organizations, such as Grammy Museum, NARAS, any non-profit organizations that offer charity to musicians, music education, etc. Beyond that, just make damn good music. That is always the best legitimizer!

So far with all this, we're planning on just going indie and doing everything ourselves as far as website, Facebook, Twitter, ad campaigns, etc., and using the site bandcamp.com to sell all this. Should I still look into trying to find a distributor/investor to put out hard copies in stores just for the sake of it being more legit?

Hard copies are so passé these days. The only folks currently in stores these days are artists who are at the top of the food chain: Beyoncé, Maroon5, Taylor Swift, Coldplay, et al. The usual suspects. Focus your attention on electronic media, and get as many hits and views as you can on all the popular sites. If you get investor money, it's better to spend it on hiring an army of kids to blog about you day and night. That provides more bang for your buck than hard copies.

As a producer, what kind of documents/agreements should I get my artist to fill out for me? This is mostly for the sake of intellectual property stuff, since money really isn't involved yet. I'm producing all the songs, but am the co-writer on some of them; I'm not sure how that will work.

Just make sure to do song-split agreements for each song you participate in. It is a simple sheet showing the splits between the writers. Remember, a song is usually divided by 50 percent "music" and 50 percent lyrics and melody. If you get anyone to perform on a production of yours, have them sign a simple work-for-hire sheet showing that they were paid for their performance, but own none of the copyright (writing).

Will the PROs take care of all the copyrighting and stuff like that for me or should I have my own stuff together also? I've copyrighted works on my own before.

The PROs will not do the copyrighting stuff. You must do that for yourself. The PROs just collect pennies for you when your music is streamed on the Internet, played in a movie, on a radio station, on TV, in a commercial, etc. You must let them know when you get a song into one of these so they can collect for you. They will not know to collect unless you tell them where your songs are placed.

Last one (this is something I'll probably call ASCAP and ask about): My artist is already registered with BMI as a writer. If I end up on ASCAP, hypothetically, is it going to be a pain in the butt to work together? Like I said, I'm co-writing a lot of this and I don't know if it's just a thing as simple as we'll be on both or if there will be a conflict with all that.

No problem whatsoever. It does not matter that you are with different PROs.

Thanks so much for the advice, Darryl. It's invaluable!

Okay, man. Holler!

QUESTION
Hello Mr. Swann,

I met you at a conference seminar in Norfolk, Virginia. I have a couple of questions. I am a music engineer and producer; I want to start a label or even help a couple of artists get on top. I believe in them and really feel like they have the sound and look to trend in the industry. I want to go the independent route; I have about $3000 right now to start to invest in the artist. I just need to know where I should start and what would be a good plan for us to get heard and build fans in this industry. He is also a hip-hop artist, but it's more of an Ab-Soul/'90s hip-hop sound. If you could help me, I would greatly appreciate it. Thank you for your time.

–Brian

ANSWER

Hey man,

What you all are doing sounds cool. So, first of all, is the recorded product industry standard? Does it stand up sonically to similar, competitive stuff out there now? Also, you need a compelling video that captures the essence of the project visually. If you are missing either of these two, then you are not ready to launch.

The video needs to capture the viewer's attention immediately, and must seamlessly match the single it is attached to. A perfect example is that Maclemore "Thrift Shop" record and visual. The viewer gets it right away; it all makes sense together. Your project has to be dialed in so tight before you go live with the website. Also, the website has to be visually stimulating and intuitive. (I'm sure you know this.) But for real, the site has to be bulletproof in terms of both look and feel.

Also, your site should be linked to a digital distribution company like TuneCore. They will shotgun spray your EP (three- to six-song product) into many of the most popular dig outlets (iTunes, et al). Do some research on Wikipedia on artists who recently have broken through. There is always a tipping-point action the artist took that got the attention of their "critical mass" fan base and allowed them to become attractive to a major, or to create new avenues for success for themselves.

Once you have all the above infrastructure stuff in place, then start gigging and trying to open up for headliner acts on tour that roll through Norfolk and the surrounding areas. Find out who the local booking agents for the arenas are. These are the folks who speak to the touring act's booking agents and actually book the date in that arena.

To restate for emphasis: It is useless to get gigs until you have the infrastructure all set up. One does gigs in order to direct eyeballs to one's website or draw attention to the project, products, and movement, which is the foundation. Your site is your home base. Without a compelling site that has a visually stimulating visual and links to activities of the artist, you have nothing.

Lastly, once this is all set up, you then need to organize a "boiler room" of folks who do nothing but chirp, tweet, and network about the project. Okay, I'm going to stop for now. Chew on this for now and let me know you got this email.
Holler,
   –Darryl Swann

p.s. I am not Mr. Swann. That is my father, Mr. David Swann Sr. I'm just Darryl.

ROYALTIES – A DIALOGUE

Hey Darryl,

Do you have a few moments to help me with something? My lawyer is on vacation, but also I don't think he will be getting back to me since my retainer is a little overdue. Your help would be most appreciated.

I'm in the middle of licensing a song to an Asian artist; I own 15 percent of it. The producer I wrote the song with is signed to BMG. His publishing is taken care of. As for me, the artist's publishers are asking me to do a sub-publishing deal with them to collect my royalties in the area they cover.

–Chara

Hi Chara,

Technically, a sub-publishing deal is if, for instance, a domestic music publisher does not have a regional office in Belgium, let's say, they will hire a local publisher in Belgium to collect in that country for them. The standard rate for the foreign, hired, collecting publisher is usually 15–25 percent, so your people seem to be asking for a fair number.

–Darryl

I always thought, up until now, that my PRO (BMI) would collect all my royalties, even internationally.

Remember, there are different types of royalties:

1. Performance royalties: These pennies are collected by your PRO (ASCAP, BMI, SESAC) from radio stations, etc. Performance royalties are when your song is played publicly – on radio, in a TV show or movie, in a nightclub, streamed, satellite, etc.

2. Mechanical royalties: These are the pennies a record company pays to the song owners/publishers each time a physical (or virtual: iTunes) record is sold. This is your royalty from the artist's label for allowing them to burn your intellectual property onto their piece of plastic (CD, download, etc.). Mechanical royalties are for the physical sale of the song to a consumer.

Your PRO will collect only your performance royalties. You or your publisher, which can be you, are responsible for collecting your mechanical royalties. Most self-publishers like yourself hire a company to collect mechanicals; this is called an administration deal. A publisher/collector usually charges three to five percent to collect for you. In your case, they are asking for 15 percent so they can enjoy the potential profits, and also collect and account for you.

Since I take care of my own publishing, I was told by the producer's publisher (BMG) that I would need to handle some paperwork on my own and track my own royalties.

They are correct in that you must track your own mechanical royalties, or hire someone to track for you, as I just explained.

It's all very vague and confusing. I have attached the sub-publishing draft I was sent from the artist's publisher (EEG) for you to look over if you have the time – or just let me know if this is beneficial to me and if the terms are standard. They are asking for 15 percent, leaving me 85 percent, and for a three-year term, I believe.

Three years is a fair term, but after that amount of time you must either ask them to continue collecting for you or hire someone else to collect for you. Usually, pop songs don't have a long life; in three years' time, all the blood has been drained from the turnip. On the other hand, if the song is a hit, or has the potential to be covered by another artist down the road, then it could have a life past these three years. Just know that after these three years are up, it is up to you to make sure someone is collecting for you on that song.

Hey lady, hit me up if you have any other questions or need any clarification. I'll hit you right back this time.

QUESTION

Hey Darryl,

I'm working with this guy I really like. He wants to have a specific kind of sound for his vocal: super-retro sounding, really garage '60s. I know I can take a few different routes, but if I were to take the mic route, would that be a ribbon mic? An old tube mic? Do you think I could get this sound with a plug-in?

Miss you, buddy! Btw, have you ever used playlist in PT to comp vocals? It's pretty killer.

–Steve

ANSWER

Hey man,

Miss you too! Did you ever go see Zombie Joe's play?

Regarding your question, if you were to go the mic route, that would be more of a ribbon mic vibe. As you know, ribbons tend to have a really flat response as they don't grab the highs really well, which gives that old sound. Funny that ribbons are what was used in the old days… so that is the sound.

Go with an old ribbon, not one of those new-fangled ribbon hybrid things that are all over the market these days. These new ones don't sound like ribbons; they sound like dynamics. They sound too good.

There are plug-ins that add to that old vintage sound:
1. Funk-logic maximizer: Just adds lo-fi noise; pretty useless for anything else.
2. Lo-fi filter plug-in: There are many out there.
3. Bit-cruncher plug: Synthetically decimates the bit rate, which gives you a grainy sound.
4. Sci-Fi plug-in: Pro Tools, another decimator of fidelity.

At the end of the day, you could use any EQ and simply filter off a little of the highs, a little of the lows, and boost the mids (2k to 4k) a few dB, then compress the hell out of it. Bam! Lo-fi. Let me know how it comes out.

Very solid article here. I agree fully. Things have a way of circling back around. Being a composer-slash-music guy, little gems and riffs of music I stumble across here and there, usually by mistake, often get used weeks, months, or even years later by me.

When I'm working on something and need a corner transition or a mood, I dig through my little "mood-riff bank" on the hard drive. There I find the perfect piece for the current work I'm crafting.

It's amazing how this always happens. It just goes to show that when you create – or stumble across – a creative gem, don't take for granted that you'll remember it again some day. Document it, then tuck it away in your creative piggy bank (on your hard drive)! That way, you'll always have a wealth of gold nuggets to draw from, which only grows as time passes.

We pull down our creative gems from the ether, from God, from the Universe – whatever one chooses to call it. You know when you've received something special because it touches you, it evokes an emotion in you, and the more you feel that "touch," the more you learn to trust your instinct. You know that "touch" means you indeed have a gem, whether it be a phrase of a lyric, a sound, a passing chord, a melody, etc.

Don't doubt your gut. I've learned that the very first thing I "feel" is my gut/heart/soul connected to all that is. The second thought is my brain, trying to analyze, dissect, and rationalize what my heart felt. Too often, if I listen to my second thought (brain), I think myself right out of a beautiful gem!

I've learned to trust my gut more and more. If I initially and immediately feel something, *I don't doubt that I felt something.* I go with it! If a bee stings me, *I got stung*, no doubt about it. It's as simple as that. So why do we doubt when we are moved/touched by a creative moment or discovery? Obviously, because creativity is sublime and subjective, as opposed to something as obvious as a bee sting. So, we must calibrate our "feeling" meters to gauge much finer readings, instead of keeping it on default.

Later,

–Darryl

QUESTION

Darryl,

Honest opinion? I think the mix down could be a little better, but it was the best he could do.

–Matt

ANSWER

I love this vibe, Matt. This is fresh. Very cool song, cool production. Your vocal tone is real radio. This is very close. The spirit is right there. The hook is dope!

The only lyric that limits the universality of the hook is the word "swag," where you say "when swag like mine starts approaching you." It is cool when you use the word in the verse because it is not such a central, important lyric. But in the hook, that spot should have a more timeless word, instead of such a trendy, cliché term as "swag." The hook is too strong to have such a semi-played-out, flavor-of-the-week word in it.

Everything is dope. That is the only thing that could limit it.

The arrangement is ill; I love how the piano follows you on the ascent in the hook. The entire hook could grow in intensity and instrumentality to sell the hook better. It is strong, but could lift even more. The vocal performance is ill, but you have more juice in you. I know you could sell the vocal even more.

Bottom line and overall: I love it. Total radio. Shit's hot. Great work, dog. I can go deeper on other things, but that is the basic framework on my thoughts.

Holler,

–DS

ACKNOWLEDGMENTS

Anyone who has written a book knows how labor intensive it is. There are many people who directly and indirectly have contributed to the creation of this book. I want to give heartfelt thanks to the following folks:

- Jeff Roberts, who practically single-handedly published the original version of this book, which enabled this new version to be published by Hal Leonard. You are a machine, my man.
- Carolyne Shapiro for being vigilant through the entire typing and editing process of both the original, self-published version, and this current one, and being a constant source of moral support.
- Phillip Gessert, who did the layout of the original version of the book. Also, Nicole Julius who typeset this new version.
- Jamie Cammon and Shaun Hillman for their photography.
- Jeff Schroedl at Hal Leonard Corporation for offering me this opportunity, and for giving me several extensions on delivery of the manuscript. Also, editor and project manager J. Mark Baker for being beyond patient with me during this entire process.
- Keith Wyatt at Musicians Institute for introducing me to Jeff at Hal Leonard.
- Dave Hampton for being a long-term comrade and showing me the ins and outs of writing a technical book.
- Tracy at Art-Share LA for giving me my first music-production teaching job back in 2006.
- Monica Mancillas, then Director of the Recording Department (RIT) for hiring me at Musician's Institute in 2007 and giving me the freedom to teach in my own personal, unorthodox way, and for not firing me on many occasions. My tenure at MI between 2007 and 2010 really allowed me to cut my teeth on honing my communication skills as an instructor.
- Pascale Cohen-Olivar, Director of Entertainment Studies at UCLA Extension for allowing me to truly spread my wings as an instructor and create unique courses.
- Eric Milos, owner and lead engineer of Clear Lake Recording Studios in North Hollywood, California for allowing me to use his studios for the majority of the pictures contained in this book. Thanks, bud.
- Also thanks to Clear Lake engineer and bud Ara Sarkisian for being a solid cat. And Andrew of Blue Rhode Studio for giving a brotha the "D-112 hook-up" rate. Also, Austin Rose for being the broseph on the last day of photos.

- Thanks to Tracy Bradford, Bob, and the folks at Audio Rents in Hollywood, California for allowing me to invade them and shoot some gear. You guys are great!
- Beth Marlis at Musicians Institute for inviting me to lecture and share my experiences with captive audiences at the Grammy Museum in downtown L.A.
- Nwaka Onwusa and Kait Stuebner at the Grammy Museum for making me feel at home and inviting me to speak to their audiences.
- Mike and Adam, owners of Paramount Recording in Hollywood, for being buds since 1994 and for opening their studios up to me for so many years and enabling me to make magic.
- David and Marilyn Swann for being the most supportive, encouraging folks one could ever have.
- Tina Sahadi and Donna Bandiera at the Burbank Library (California), Buena Vista Branch for being great friends and constant sources of encouragement. You're the best.
- John Guggenheim for giving me my first engineer/runner job at Silverlake Recording Studios and teaching me not to ask L.A. Reid and Babyface a million questions during my first session as they recorded the '80s hit "Rock Steady."
- Lastly, all the thousands of students I've had the pleasure of sharing with over the years. I've learned so much from all your probing questions and listening to your projects and works. Remember, I'm not the Ministry of Information; I just have a few more stab wounds than most of you guys. We are always students of the craft, no matter how many accolades one possesses.

ABOUT THE AUTHOR

Darryl Swann – record producer, engineer, mixer, songwriter, educator, and musician – has worked with many prominent artists, including Macy Gray, The Black Eyed Peas, and Mos Def. He has also had the pleasure of working with professionals such as Rick Rubin, Dave Pensado, and Dave Way. Darryl has done substantial work for Sony Records and Universal Records.

Born and raised in the Cleveland area, Darryl's fascination with music production began when, at age nine, he read the book *Modern Recording Techniques*. He played lead guitar in the garage band The Lab Rats and mixed live sound for many Cleveland area bands throughout his teenage years. After graduating from Shaker Heights High School in 1983, Swann moved to Los Angeles with the band Haven, then acquired his Liberal Arts degree from the University of California at Los Angeles (UCLA).

Swann teaches music production at several notable schools, including Musicians Institute, The Grammy Museum, Garnish Music Academy, and UCLA. His music has been heard on a number of movies and television shows, including *Spider-Man*, *Bridget Jones's Diary*, MTV's *True Life*, NBC's *Las Vegas*, ESPN's *Extreme 16* and *Core Culture*, and in commercials for Pepsi, Mountain Dew, Honda, Motorola's Razor phone, and the Apple iPhone.

Darryl also develops video games and is currently working on a ground-breaking sound-distribution algorithm and music-delivery system through his partnership with SpeakerWrap, LLC. He lives in Los Angeles.